Becoming God

A Book By FORD

Becoming God™

Drof Publishing, LLC

Drof Music, FORD Productions, LLC

www.BecomingGod.org

www.FordRecords.com

Copyright © 2005 Drof Publishing, LLC
Revised Edition © 2007

All Rights reserved. No part of this book, in part or in whole, may be reproduced, transmitted, or utilized in any form or by any means, electronic or mechanical, including photocopying, recording, or by any information storage and retrieval system, without permission in writing from the publisher, except for brief quotations in critical articles, books and reviews.

International Standard Book Number: 978-0-6151-4962-2

Cover Design By Richard Toelanie
For more artwork of higher consciousness,
please visit www.3datelier.com

Address all inquiries to:
Email: info@becominggod.org
Website: http://www.becominggod.org

For my wife, Lisa.
Thank you for your encouragement and belief in me.
It is through you that I have discovered how to live the fullest life possible.

I'll love you forever and a day…

Preface

This is not a motivational book or a religious book, nor is this a book about science. Those who have already read this have picked it to be one or the other and some have chosen it to be all three. I say to the reader, this book is whatever you want it to be. The funny thing is, this spiritually enlightening book ironically began as a book to debunk spirituality through science (I think anyone can find the humor in this). I was not the authority on this subject when I began, but I believe I am now. Upon reading this book, you will notice that my perspective and self-worth issues have changed for the better during the course of my writing. With newfound confidence and invigoration, by the time I had finished writing this book, I had discovered all of the self-worth that I could ever need as a human being. I found this undiscovered self-worth within myself and understood it to be infinitely abundant and thus I am now able to give it away.

We have become a society so distracted by technological advances and on demand entertainment that we have become isolated and disconnected. We forgot to ask questions and talk about meaningful things to raise our conscious level and our self-awareness. My message, at its core, is to get people to start talking again and recognize their infinite self-worth just as I did so that they too can ask the nest question. This book will continue to evolve and we will constantly have new ideas about what people should get out of reading it; this is something that I have struggled with now for two years. I realize however, in order to change the world, people have to begin reading it. There has to be a cut-off point; and so this revised edition is it. I would like to thank everyone who has helped me make this dream of changing the world a possibility. Together we will find our way to manifest the most fantastic dream ever dreamt, to live in a Utopian world. Anything is possible if we continue to believe that it is.

My most sincere thanks to Abraham, Roger Banister, O.R. Bontrager, Neils Bohr, Brahma, Buddha, Carlos Casteneda, Deepak Chopra, Jesus Christ, Rene Descartes, David Deutsch, Joseph Dispenza, Wayne Dyer, Albert Einstein, Hugh Everette, John Gribbin, Amit Goswami, John Hagelin, Stephen Hawking, Albert Hofmann, Carl Jung, Michio Kaku, Ray Kurzweil, John Lennon, Lynne McTaggart, Moses, Muhammad, Isaac Newton, Norman Peale, Karl Popper, Ramtha, Anthony Robbins, Carl Sagan, Jeffrey Satinover, Erwin Schrödinger, Alexander Shulgrin, Frank Tippler, Robert A. Wilson, Fred Alan Wolf and anyone else who inspired me with your work and whom I unintentionally forgot to thank.

Thank you for teaching and inspiring me to think outside of the box. Thank you for encouraging me to ask the next question. It is through the metaphors that you have unraveled, that "I" have become self-aware.

Introduction:
Your Boundless Possibility

Chapter 1: My Search For Higher Consciousness
How I Learned To Let Go of My Atheist Roots

Chapter 2: The Many Worlds Theory
The Science Behind Divine Intervention

Chapter 3: Redefining Reality
How This New Understanding Will Change Your Life

Chapter 4: How and Why
The Scientific Interpretation

Chapter 5: Having Faith In Science
Understanding The Basis For The Theories and Further Speculation

Chapter 6: Religion
The Religious Interpretation

Chapter 7: Spiritually Tying It All Together
The Unification That Can Change The World

Chapter 8: Welcome To You
Discovering The Dreaming Self and Understanding Your Life's Purpose

Chapter 9: Manifesting Your Reality
Practical Exercises To Show You That You Master Your Own Reality

Chapter 10: Manifesting Techniques
Meditation, Visualization, The Law of Attraction and Lucid Dreaming

Chapter 11: Conclusion
Defining The Dream, Defining God

"We are pure imagination. Life is the expression of the possibilities of our imagination that exceed our comprehension."

Introduction
Your Boundless Possibility

I am not a doctor or a scientist. I don't have a wall of diplomas or a list of credentials to fill the back cover of this book, nor am I a bible toting preacher or a friendly Christian trying to save you from an eternity of damnation. The purpose of this book is not to initiate a new cult or religion, but if you want to send me money, I will gladly accept your donation. I'm not a tree hugging "new age-ie" although I always thought that some of those concepts had microscopic notions of merit and that the music is nice to listen to on a rainy day. I am not a millionaire dressed in an expensive suit walking over hot coals to teach you how to exceed your monthly sales quota. I am also not a writer. Yet, here I have written a book with absolutely no concept of how to do so and you are holding the manifestation of my dream in your hands.

How is this possible? What could possibly give me the idea that I had the power and ability to sit down and write a book? I can barely read more than a page at a time without my mind drifting off into a nether world construed by my A.D.D. How could I possibly think that I possessed the ability to coherently construct sentences in a meaningful way or the audacity to think that someone else would be interested in what I have to say? Furthermore, I have no connections in the literary world. I am not a writer by trade, nor am I a writer pouring my heart into a life's work hoping for the chance to one day become published. I am none of these things. In fact, I have not even begun writing the first chapter in this book and yet, I see you with a paperback copy of it. You are a stranger to me. You are holding my completed book in your hand and you are reading it. You are absorbing what I have to say because I have demonstrated to you that my suggestions and methods to fulfilling your dreams actually work. You are holding the proof in your hand. I visualized, despite my shortcomings, the finality of this project in my mind and now it has come to fruition. I visualize, as I write these words, a picture of you. You are reading this very passage. I visualize that I have now fulfilled my dream of *teaching* you something that will forever change your life at every level of existence, consciously and unconsciously. Some may argue that I have manifested nothing extraordinary, that I set a goal and completed the necessary tasks to obtain it. I say, a goal is a dream and that the mind makes no distinction between the ordinary and the extraordinary dreams.

This may sound like an ominous introduction to a rather typical motivational book, but unlike those philosophies, here we are going to closely examine the motivation and mechanism behind those motivational thoughts and commands, diving deep into the very motive and purpose of our existence.

It turns out, the true power of the mind just may be greater than any of us ever imagined. It is certainly possible that we could very well be at the threshold of the Age of Aquarius: a union of science and spirituality and the next evolutionary jump of human reasoning; an expansion of the mind that awakens us to the realization that our thoughts not only have control over our surroundings, but that our thoughts *are* our surroundings. This is a concept that first washes over us with hardly a consideration. It is an absurd idea, one that sounds more like fantasy than it does reality. But, as you will learn in this book, there is absolutely no distinction between either realm. The true nature of reality is that it is equally as fluid as the dream world as it is tangible as the real world. To place more importance on either one would be to miss the point entirely.

This new philosophy is in its infancy and it is based on a science that is perhaps decades away from being completely understood. The implications of these concepts shatter everything we have come to understand about the nature of everything and driven the smartest men in the world to near madness. The purpose of this book is to shed some light on this very complicated science and offer a philosophy to coincide with it. The philosophy itself is fluid by design, and offered for the purpose of opening a layman's dialog on what could very well be the single greatest discovery of the human species. A discovery that redefines everything we know about everything and affects each of us individually at every level of our existence.   The intention of this book is to start a conversation about these ideas; for it is within this conversation that we become self-aware.

Although I had a general idea, I wasn't sure exactly how I was going to write this book or how I was going to convey the message that I was intending to deliver. The message is a powerful one but the concept can only be truly comprehended after intensely studying the nature of its mechanics. Only then can you harness the mind-blowing possibilities that come with this powerful notion. The concept and philosophy of this book is simple to get across but getting a reader to a state of mind where they will be open to these extreme ideas is slightly more complicated. Reaching this state of sincere open mindedness requires a complex understanding of a

Introduction

science that is in almost every way counter-intuitive. I only knew that I wanted to write the book that I had been searching for myself, a book that contemplates a radical new philosophy without meaningless metaphysical rhetoric and complicated mathematics. With that being said, it is important that you do not skip around this book. However tedious, it is the details of each idea presented in this book that will eventually lay the groundwork for your new understanding of everything. This book will at times contradict itself, however these contradictions are necessary for explaining a physics that has no rational. My only requirement is that you are committed to this book. It is only within the last chapter that you will truly find your empowerment and life's purpose. However, the only way to understand and appreciate this new found enlightenment is by fully understanding every chapter leading up to it.

So what is this book about exactly? This book is about examining the most important questions you have ever had in your life. Everyone yearns to understand the meaning of life. Everyone is deeply perplexed about who or what God is, where we came from, and where we are going when we die. These are important questions and we shouldn't feel bad for asking them nor exploring different ideas about them. On the contrary, we should only feel bad for not exploring them. I cannot think of a more profound question than what could possibly be the meaning and purpose of our existence? Religion teaches us that everything just "is" and science longs to discover "why". At the end of this book you will have a clearer understanding that both camps are right. You will understand *why* it just *is*. Beyond this, asking these questions and

Becoming God

exploring the answers will enable you to gain a completely different view of your life. For the first time, you will have control over your destiny in a far more profound way than you ever thought possible. This book will present to you a scientific analysis of the mechanics of the meaning of life. By understanding the mechanics of how something works we can maintain it, fix it and fine-tune it for the highest performance possible. What I mean by the mechanics of the meaning of life is having a clear understanding of our purpose and the mechanism guiding us towards it. As I will show you in this book, your being or existence is no accident and you do serve a purpose within the universe. You contribute through thought and action to an ever-growing mind, the mind of the universe itself.

More than this, this book is about giving you what you have been missing in your life. This book is going to take you on a mind-numbing journey closely examining and further developing a philosophy from today's most cutting edge science and technology. By bringing together the resent discoveries in quantum physics, cosmology, neurobiology and computation with ancient philosophies, spirituality and religion, this book is going to bring you the sense of wonder, awe and direction that you have been searching for. You will learn a new appreciation for life and the meaning of it all. Never before has there been a more thought provoking idea than what these resent discoveries have asked us to consider.

The recent discoveries in quantum physics are among the greatest realizations in human history. Despite the magnitude of this, there are no parades, no continuous news coverage of the

Introduction

unfolding events, nor White House interruptions. There is no excitement whatsoever because the implications of these discoveries are so mind blowing few can fully comprehend it and even fewer are willing to accept it. These discoveries arguably tower over the significance of the endeavors of Columbus, Pasture, Einstein, or any other historical giant or unforgettable moments in history. They are discoveries that shatter every concept we have of the reality in which we live and affect us all more profoundly than anything else we have ever encountered.

This is not a religion nor is it science fiction, it is a radical concept and it is a way of life. It is a new way of looking at things. What I am going to open your mind to is not something for you to cherish or worship, it is something for you to think about, understand scientifically, and develop for yourself. I am going to teach you how to tap into an infinite source of knowledge and power equal to God. The connection is already there and you are already using it. This book is going to make you consciously aware of it and show you how to use it to its fullest potential.

Imagine that you are a computer and your Ethernet port is connected to an infinitely powerful Internet. This Internet is special, its knowledge and possibilities are limitless. Guidance and information to anything you can imagine, no matter how specific, are at your virtual fingertips. Through this Internet you will be able to easily locate and access the drivers or "drive" to any mental or physical program or skill set you wish to run or accomplish. You will be able to easily locate and access protection against and remedies to any virus that ails you physically. By just running the program you will heal yourself. Again, there are no limits here. If

Becoming God

it is your wish to defy gravity and fly like superman, simply locate the program, run it and it will happen.

Right now you're probably thinking this is all just a bunch of meta-physical new age bull and wondering when I'm going to ask you to light a money candle or enter your credit card number on this magical super-duper information highway. You're thinking, what kind of an asshole promises the sky? Believe me, I have been in your shoes. I have shared those thoughts. When I was first introduced to these concepts I passed it off as rubbish too. These are not my teachings or ideas. These are ancient ideas. They are ideas that have been around for a long, long time but somehow got lost in all of the hype that came with it. Somewhere along the way the idea itself was left behind and only the hype continued on to be worshiped and praised.

The idea that I am talking about encompasses the Law of Attraction, the Power of Suggestion and the Power of Belief. The idea is about asking your subconscious mind to tap into a source of knowledge and power and simply instructing it to download and run your desired programs. The programs are already there you just need to learn how to search for them and use them.

There are hundreds of self-help books and other media available teaching these techniques because the techniques work. However, getting the techniques to work relies on a single principle and that is you must *believe* that they work. These teachings are much like a placebo, where in they are only effective if you truly believe without a shred of doubt that they are working. Any doubt whatsoever in the power of your positive suggestion breaks the communication process between your conscious and subconscious mind. The other self help books also agree with this, but they still fail to sufficiently address our doubts perpetuating, at least for many of us, a technique that does not work.

There are many people who are comfortable accepting new ideas on blind faith just as there are many people who need emphatical evidence before accepting anything. Whichever kind of person you are, this book is going to improve your ability to successfully implement the power of suggestion and belief because this book is going to explain to you the mechanics of how this process works. This is something nobody else has been able to do before now. By understanding the mechanics of the process, any lingering doubt that you may have will recede. The communication process between your conscious and subconscious mind will become unblocked and the true power of your mind will become apparent to you.

Understanding the mechanics of the process however, is irrational and nearly impossible to comprehend without first giving up every preconceived notion you have about yourself and the nature of reality. Although this practice has been around for centuries, until recently nobody has had an explanation for why the process works; which is why many people have passed this notion off as magic or coincidence, or anything but scientific. With our new understanding of reality however, a new philosophy of the world is being developed. A philosophy that is radically different from our present understanding of everything. However impossible this philosophy appears to be, it answers nearly all of our scientific questions as well as the deepest questions harbored

Becoming God

inside each one of us and it enlightens us to the awesome power that each of us has over our own lives. As radical as this philosophy is, it is majestic, beautiful and it could very well be the answer to creating a Utopian world.

Now that I have presented the limitless possibilities to you, I am going to take you away from all of it because the only way to get there is to come to these conclusions on your own. Taking my word for it does not work. It is your belief that is the key to its success. As I said before, I am a skeptic and you should be too! You should doubt anyone who comes to you with ideas as preposterous as these. Denying these notions, examining the evidence, exploring theories and making your own conclusions are how you satisfy your core belief system. Do not under any circumstances just accept these ideas on blind faith alone. Blind faith is the reason the teachings have failed us thus far. You need to not believe in any other possibility. No matter how much you say you believe in the power of suggestion or the power of "God", if it isn't working for you it is because you have doubts.

"If a man will begin with certainties, he will end in doubts; but if he will be content to begin with doubts he will end in certainties."

~Francis Bacon

Chapter 1:

My Search For Higher Consciousness

How I Learned To Let Go of My Atheist Roots

Becoming God

Throughout this book I am going to make some very outlandish and possibly blasphemous remarks. If you can get through it without feeling like I am damned for writing it and you are damned for reading it, then you are ready and your mind is opening. This is the first step in the right direction. As blasphemous as much of it may be, in many ways we will come full circle. However, the only way to complete this circle is to open your mind to any possibility and clear it of any preconceptions.

Religion has brainwashed us, not necessarily in a bad or "sinister" way but certainly in a counter productive way. I promise you that when you finish this book and apply the philosophy you will feel as I did, robbed of so many years of your life. You will think about what you may have been able to accomplish if you had only been taught this at an earlier age. If you grew up in a religious home, more than likely you were taught these ideologies. However, you were asked to accept the teachings on blind faith, which as you will learn in this book, is one of the fundamental flaws in religion. From the first time you heard that Jonah rode inside of a whale's mouth or that Moses parted the Red Sea and countless other stories of the bible, no matter how devoted you were to the religion there was a seed of doubt planted in your mind at a subconscious level. You never even noticed it was there, a dark lurking shadow over the religion. Stories that were just counter intuitive. Your brain, despite your agreement to accept things on blind faith, just could not accept these things as real. The seed of doubt subtly grew to work against everything else you were being taught.

In this chapter, I am going to tell you about how I was introduced to these ideas and tell you how my embracing these concepts forever changed my life just as learning these philosophies will forever change your life. My purpose for this chapter, other than for a little self-indulgence, is to demonstrate to you that if a cynical Atheist like me can open my closed mind to these radical concepts than so can you.

I am a skeptic. I always have been. I am or was a self proclaimed Agnostic. You could really call me an Atheist but that is such a dirty word. If you really want to loose your friends in a hurry just say that you're an Atheist and watch them run. I know people with 666 tattooed to their foreheads that had more friends. The difference is a Satan worshiper believes in something. Belief is all you need in this world and beliefs can be persuaded. An Atheist needs proof. They need to see it in black & white without a hint of gray. People with blind faith have a hard time dealing with someone who is unable to take that leap. They see it as a mental illness. It's scary to them, far scarier than the devil himself because they cannot relate, they cannot argue and there is no hope of persuading you into accepting their beliefs.

The trouble with being an Atheist is that it gets boring. Atheists are waiting for the data to come in and explain it all. The problem is the proof is never going to come. The evidence for the meaning of life can be thoroughly examined and traced back in time and space to more than 15 billion years ago, macro seconds

Becoming God

after the Big Bang and that's where everything breaks down. There are no calculations, sophisticated mathematics or physics to be studied that can give us any hint of where all of this, our universe comes from. What kind of a way is that to live? Accepting the fact that there isn't going to be any answers to anything until we die? There still isn't any indication that someone or something jumps out and hands us "The Answers to Everything" book then either. What fun is that?

I have since found religion to be so on point with the true meaning of life, and I think that it can truly make ones life better. However, there are severe problems with religion (and I'm talking about nearly all of them). One of the problems is that there seems to be too much emphasis on the worshiping of the messengers and not enough emphasis on the message itself. In two thousand years there has been virtually no development of these ideologies, but instead intense scrutiny over the life and death of the messengers. For example, I recently saw Mel Gibson's "Passion of the Christ", a 3 hour film about a guy getting tortured to death. There is almost no dialog in this film. The historical figure that the movie is about had so many insightful and incredible ideas and none of them appeared in this film. The vary symbol for Christianity itself is the crucifix, the device used to torture Jesus to death. Religion seems to be missing the point.

Still another problem with religion is they all get hung up on details. They hold sacred and take literally things that are just not so. In the words of Dr. Carl Sagan, "Evolution is not a theory, it is a fact. It really happened." The Earth is not 6,000 years old, not in today's numerical system or in any ancient calendars or math either. The church wants to know why attendance is declining and this is a big part of the answer. There are too many of us, especially the younger generations, who have grown up with so much contradictory information readily available to us. Let's face it, dinosaur bones are not fossils put here by God to test our faith. Which is the Vatican's official position. No, they are the fossils of bones of creatures that lived and breathed and dominated the earth for a million times longer than man has even contemplated it. What is the harm in accepting this? Why can't the church just admit that there were some things, incorrect facts and embellishments, added to the bible to give it some flare, so that it would appeal to the masses? After all, it is the greatest story ever told; does it all have to be true?

The insightfulness and teachings of Jesus Christ as with the messengers of other religions are awe inspiring and I never learned about any of it in Catholic school. Why? Because I was too hung up on the ridiculous customs, rules, guilt and fictional stuff they were teaching. How could I pay any attention to the teachings of this Jesus fellow when I couldn't get past all of the other misinformation being passed off as fact? The Catholics were teaching me facts that contradicted what I was learning outside of the Church and the real truth provided me with evidence not blind faith. The truly sad part is I had to become an adult Atheist to learn about the teachings of Jesus Christ, Buddha, Moses, Abraham, Muhammad, and countless other incredibly wise people. These people made a lasting impact on the world because they had an idea that strongly affected the people they preached to; and despite the fact that religions have since built walls of misinformation

Becoming God

around each of these wise souls along with their ideas to separate them from one another, is they all shared a similar notion. What was so fantastic about their ideas, that got people to embrace them as Gods, were their fundamental ideas, when applied and practiced, brought results. The application of positive thinking and the power of belief is the most brilliant discovery of all time.

I was introduced to these philosophies at an early age, like many of you, through religion. I was raised Catholic. My mother was devoutly religious and my father, though he believed in God and the teachings of the Bible, was not a church going man. I grew up in a fascinating time in our history. Man had just walked on the moon; we had just landed two spacecrafts on nearby planets and sent another spacecraft out of the solar system carrying with it a message in the event the spacecraft was picked up by beings from another world. This was tough competition for the church. In my room I had astronaut wallpaper, stacks of books about space and a model of the solar system. I would attend catechism with my space books and I drew pictures of alien landscapes when I should have been listening. When I asked about aliens and if Jesus had visited them, I was scornfully quieted down. There was simply no room in the bible or church for that matter for alien beings and the wonders of the universe. From then on church became a chore to me, like going to school. Something you just had to do. My faith had become less than whole hearted.

After a brief stint of disenchantment with my faith, I was introduced to these philosophies again in my teens. I was an underachiever. School and pretty much life itself bored me. Like most teens I was consumed with depression and video games. When I was fifteen, my parents got me some tapes by the personal power guru, Tony Robbins. Mr. Robbins had a bunch of really exciting ideas that he was evidently really fired up about! Anything is possible, he said if you put your mind to it! Blah, blah, blah. My seed of doubt had grown so big it consumed the entire open area of my brain. All of the years of empty promises by religion, my parents, schoolteachers, product advertisements and so on had taken a toll on the wisdom that lay inside my mind. This guy was as full of crap as everyone else, I thought. Without even considering his message he was dismissed in my mind. This man was talking about core beliefs and the powers of suggestion but he failed, at least with me, in satisfying and changing my core beliefs. His sales pitch did not work because he did not first break through my cynicism to eliminate my ever-growing seed of doubt. Not only did my cynicism keep me from having an open mind it blocked me from even hearing the message. In my mind, this guy had a good scam going. He was good at it. His enthusiasm was nothing short of spectacular. He was an amazing speaker and salesman. But that is what he remained to me, a salesman.

I look back and think if only I had appreciated what he was so enthusiastic about then how different my life would be today. But, he did not sell me. My cynicism was like a scar, and the more people I met who bought into his words just made me more confident in my beliefs. Most of the people I met were so quick to rattle off his sayings but few if any applied them. The hypocrisy reminded me of the church. Today, I hold a very different opinion of him.

Becoming God

This is what we need to get passed with you in this book. Right now, your cynicism is telling you that there is no way I can fulfill the claims that I have made. To you, I am just someone who wrote a book to get published to make money. Maybe my sentiments are sincere and my intentions are good you think, but there is just no way its going to have any significance on your life. I am telling you it can and it will have a mind blowing significant impact on your life once we remove that seed of doubt that is compromising the true power of your mind. The power that lies inside your mind can move mountains, literally. Believe me, I know how ridiculous this sounds to you. I have been where you are. Every conceivable possibility is obtainable to you. All you have to do is believe that is.

After my abandonment of the church and my rejection of Tony Robbins, I was left meandering about without a clue as to what I was supposed to be doing with my life. I was a mental rebel in my youth, nothing to brag about, but I found just about anything with a hint of authority disconcerting. I was an intellect, although my grades never reflected that, and I tended to question everything. I found conspiracy and cynicism everywhere I looked, and I reveled in the fact that I knew and understood it all so clearly and just couldn't grasp how everyone else could be so naive.

I went on for years that way. God forbid if my mother ever learned my true feelings. She knew I wasn't very committed to my faith, but had no idea how strongly opposed I was to it. About this time I met a friend who introduced me to Judaism. There were some interesting concepts here. It wasn't much different than Catholicism at the core; well, except for the Jesus part. I was pleased that there was no Hell in Judaism. I always thought that a vindictive God would be counter productive and figured that if there was an all knowing God out there he would be smarter than that. After all, he made us the way we were didn't he? In addition to this, being "all knowing" meant that he could see the future, see what would become of us before it happened. If we were to throw our lives away doing bad things, to the point that he needed to punish us eternally for it, why wouldn't he just not create us to begin with and save the energy? Yes I know, I over think a lot of things but I am fun at parties.

Judaism was an interesting concept but I found many of the same fundamental flaws in it as I did with Catholicism. They too were stuck on details, obsessed with the stories and the fabricated histories. There was no room in that religion either for the wonders of space. From then on I didn't give religion or divinity much thought. I was an Atheist. Of course, I would never admit that to anyone, but in the right social crowd it was cool to say I was Agnostic. For me, the jury was still out. I would have to admit there was always a very small section in my mind holding out for God, just in case... When times got bad I made short little prayers to my self and when things went exceptionally right I would thank God. Old habits die hard I guess. I wasn't a very devoted Atheist in practice either.

Before I continue on with my story of how I re-discovered the powers of the universe and how I eliminated my seeds of doubt, I wanted to qualify this section of the book. I want to ease any animosity you might be feeling as you read. Some of you might be at a place in your life not too different from what I just described.

Becoming God

If you are, then I know you really don't want to hear about all of this religious garbage. I promise you this book is not about religion. This is not a trick, where I am going to ask you to become a born again Christian or anything of the sort. I am telling you this part because I need to convince you that I understand how you are feeling and that I can relate. Atheists are always searching.

In further chapters I will be going into great detail with regards to the mechanics of how the process works. Things will get extremely scientific. We will examine everything from neurobiology to physics, quantum mechanics, cosmology, quantum cosmology, psychology, philosophy and (less scientifically) metaphysics. All of this will be to eliminate your seeds of doubt. But before we get to those sections, you need to come to them with an open mind just as I did. We need to eliminate or at least reduce your cynicism towards the ideas that lie outside of your box. You need to be at a point in your life where you are willing to accept new ideas by considering the theory and weighing it against the evidence.

This goes the same for anyone reading this that is still holding on to their religious beliefs. Whether or not you agree with my youthful opinions with regards to religion, you cannot argue that you have accepted your beliefs on blind faith and blind faith alone. The bible, in all of its variations, as with all other religious doctrine are in the end, just stories written down by mortal men; Men with a brain no different from yours writing about the unknowable. There is absolutely no credible evidence to back up anything at the core of any religion.

My Search For Higher Consciousness

At the end of this book, those of you who are holding on to your religious beliefs will get to keep them; At least the core ideology. But first you must abandon those beliefs entirely and approach this with an open mind. Don't just say that you are abandoning it you have to do it. I promise the devil isn't going to get you! You have to accept the fact that your beliefs currently rest on the shoulders of blind faith and further accept that as wonderful and comforting as your religion might be to you, you will always have that seed of doubt at the core of your subconscious. In other words, you think you believe in your religion, but the truth is you cannot believe in any religion and at the same time be a rational thinking being. Soon you will look at your beliefs in a whole new way. For the first time in your life you will understand the core of your religion and you will accept it and embrace it without your doubts interfering. All of the hype surrounding the religions that were put in place to attract more followers will be gone. The core of all religion is eloquent, it is beautiful and it is simple. The fact is, most religions can be chiseled down to a few short ideas: You have the power to make whatever you wish of your life. You have the power to do anything that you desire and there are no limitations to that power. You are directly connected to an infinitely powerful, all knowing "God" because you and it are one.

I was never a popular person growing up. I wasn't a jock or cool, but I wasn't a nerd either. I was just a ghost. Not having a lot of friends left me alone to entertain myself. I was fascinated with computers, but not enough to be a considered a computer geek. Who knows what would have happened if I had gotten a computer of my own, but that wouldn't be until late into college. Computers were rare in those days maybe one or two kids on the block had one. At the time they seemed to function only slightly more than as glorified typewriters. They played games too, but Atari was much better for that.

Instead I had a different hobby. I was a drummer. I got a drum kit when I was really young and I loved to pound out beats along with my Dad who would play rocked out guitar riffs on the electric guitar. My interest in music merged with my interest in computers, which led me eventually to the synthesizer, an electronic keyboard capable of making all kinds of unique and interesting sounds.

I fantasized about one day being a rock star. Duran Duran was big at the time and the idea of being someone like a Nick Rhodes was the ultimate fantasy. Everyone has fantasies of fame and fortune at one time or another in their lives but for me it was different. I don't think I ever really believed that it would happen, however, there was definitely a connection there that haunted me. The thoughts and fantasy of making records and being on the radio consumed me. I didn't become obsessed with it because I was brought up in a very conservative family. Not that dreams were squashed in my family, but dreams like those were just dreams. Rationally, I needed to make plans to go to college and then on to a respectable career.

So, I focused on my duty; school, barely I might add, but I pushed through it because I knew in my family there wasn't going to be much of a choice. I continued on with my music as well. As a wanna-be computer geek, and my fascination with gadgets, I decided to pursue a career as an airline pilot. Being around all of those knobs and switches just seemed natural. It just *"felt right"*.

Everyone has experienced this feeling in their lives but have they ever stopped to really think about where that feeling comes from? We've all experienced at one time or another that strange feeling of familiarity and comfort like we belong there or, have even been there before. Most of the time we dismiss the feeling without reading much into it. We chalk it up to "déjà vu ", or call it "gut instinct" or "women's intuition". It is only when the feelings won't let go of us that we follow those feelings to see where they leads us. Why? Why do we wait so long? Why isn't it an acceptable part of our culture to go with all of those feelings and see where they lead us? The feelings are there for a reason. Whether or not the feeling is there because it is part of some deep seeded psychological issue or there because your subconscious has tapped into a source of knowledge and is now guiding you, the feelings are there and they should be explored. Why is this frowned upon in our society? Why is this considered a waste of time? Why is there such little importance placed on following your heart, following your gut instincts and curiosities?

Think about how different your life would be if you followed your gut instincts regardless of consequence. Maybe you would have been more successful or perhaps not. But either way you would be on a completely different path. Now put that into perspective with the meaning of life. If you do have a purpose, do you think that you are now on the road that you were supposed to be on? These feelings come from your subconscious mind, which is connected to and a part of an infinitely powerful and all knowing

Becoming God

entity, our source. Your subconscious knows where it is leading you. Although it may sometimes look wrong to you, your subconscious is guiding you ultimately to the correct road. Like a chess game of life, your subconscious is plotting out moves millions of steps in advance and recommending those moves to you. All you have to do is listen to the advice being whispered to your conscious self. To your subconscious, the game has already been played in its entirety and it is simply retracing the steps. The moves necessary for the perfect win are already there. They have already been played.

Flight school was intense and difficult for me. It required a lot of studying and a lot of hard work. The difference was in school if you did poorly you just got a bad grade. In flight school if you did not study you could hurt or even kill yourself. It was stressful for me. I had hardly studied a day in my life for anything until now and this was taking a toll on me. To compound the issue, I was living in a new city and I had no friends. To relieve the stress and loneliness I had answered an ad in the paper from a band seeking a keyboard player. I don't know why I did it. I certainly did not have time for it. If there was ever a time in my life where I did not need hobbies or friends to distract me than this was it. However, something drew me to the ad; something pushed me to make the call. I can't say that I had given in to my subconscious thoughts cognitively. I didn't give much thought to it at all; I just did it. Years later I would look back at that moment, wondering where I would be today had I not answered the ad. Would I have answered another ad? Would I have focused on school? It was a pivotal point in my life, one of many. We all encounter points like these numerous times throughout our lives. Think for a second about similar moments in your life. Go back and imagine yourself taking a different path. Where do you think you would be?

I joined the band and it really made me happy. It was also a great stress reliever. We practiced a few times together and things just clicked. I also liked the people I was around. They were older than me by a number of years. They introduced me to a new crowd, an "artsy" crowd. There were countless nights at coffee houses where groups of them went on endlessly in meta-physical talk and new age practices. I thought these people were just as whacked as the devout Christians but at least they followed their own ideology, which I thought was very courageous and interesting. It was nice to be a part of a crowd that certainly didn't frown upon anyone's beliefs. It was perfectly okay in this circle to be Agnostic. Atheism would still be pushing it.

For the first time in my life I began to think about my beliefs. I didn't have any. To me there was absolutely no room for God. Everything, I thought could be explained by the forces of nature and with sciences we just didn't understand yet. I imagined that one day we would make contact with an alien civilization and they would have to gently let everyone down who were still holding on to their religious beliefs. "This is how it all works," they would tell us. For me, there was no magic in the universe; there was hardly a mystery. Being an Atheist got lonely sometimes. If I found myself in crisis, surely out of habit, I would pray in search of an answer only to think to myself how ridiculous the idea was, and hence break down any hope that the prayer may have brought me. Why would God answer someone who didn't believe?

Months went by and some of the New Age stuff was beginning rub off on me. I found myself thinking about my decisions and considering how my decisions affected the balance and harmony around me. Could all of this be on purpose I thought? Could it be possible that there was somehow a grand plan that was focusing the direction of my life? The idea was counter-intuitive and just flat out goofy, but somehow it was comforting. For the first time in my life I was a true Agnostic. I still didn't believe in anything, but I was open to suggestion.

Around this time I was introduced to Buddhism. I made it clear that I was against any kind of organized religion but I was open to hearing about the core of the belief. The core of Buddhism, I found, is pretty straightforward but extremely profound. It can be summed up in two simple phrases. "Do good" and "Be good". Buddhism was about listening to yourself and following your heart. It was about being good to your self and being good to others (an oxymoron my cynicism was telling me). The idea had nice qualities though. Even if I didn't whole-heartedly believe in them, I felt that following this path was a good thing. I wanted to be good. Maybe if I were good, good things would happen to me. It was certainly more interesting and fun than being an Atheist; but those silly robes were just not an option.

After a few months, my band was ready to record our first demo. I had never recorded a demo before. The other guys had been down this road countless times. They suggested that we all work hard and contributed our money together until we had saved up enough money to go into a professional recording studio to record the demo.

The day came to record and something strange happened. I experienced an uncanny feeling of déjà vu the moment I walked into the control room of the recording studio. It was like the cockpit of an airplane, there were gadgets and switches everywhere I looked. The dim lighting, cedar wood walls and general atmosphere were comfortable to me. It felt like I was coming home after being away at college for a very long time. It was like re-entering the womb. Everything just felt comfortably right. I knew, without a shadow of doubt that I was supposed to be there. The feeling consumed me the entire time I was there.

After a few days our session was complete and we had our demo. I couldn't believe it! We had our own tape. I could listen to music by my favorite artist and then listen to the music of my own. It was remarkable. A few months went by, and I couldn't seem to ease the nagging sensation and need to be in that recording studio. Eventually, I went back and offered to help out for free. I asked if I could get an unsanctioned internship with them. Somehow I didn't think that my school advisors were going to grant me a real internship at a recording studio based on the fact that both airplanes and recording studios had a lot of buttons and switches. It didn't matter. Being a studio slave would be just fine for a while.

That summer I went home for a couple of weeks. I drove my car back to Atlanta for about 15 hours all the time listening to my three-song demo tape. When I got home I played it for my family and everyone was enthusiastic. I had a couple of friends back home that I also played it for. One of my friends had an older brother who was almost famous. He was a guitar player and singer/songwriter who was famous around town. He had gotten a record deal a few years before and was even on MTV a few times. He was a one hit wonder, but around town he was still very well known. As I was playing my tape for my friend his brother walked in the room. He told me he was very impressed with the sound. He thought that it really had potential. This struck an incredible chord with me. This guy was so admired for his musical ability and he was telling me that I had the goods. I got goose bumps and couldn't believe what I was hearing. Everyone thinks that their stuff is great, whether it's your art, athletic ability, work or music or whatever. If you are lucky enough to have a good family and good friends then they are going to tell you that you are great too. I hardly knew this guy! What I did know however was that he wasn't the type to give out praise very freely. I had met him countless times before and I could probably count the number of words he said to me on one hand in all of those encounters. His praise that day gave me a kind of courage and confidence that I had never felt before.

As I drove home, all I could think about was how everything was clicking for me. I thought about the feelings that were nagging at me. I thought about my new exploration in alternative thinking and philosophy. And I also thought about where my life was going. I was nearly two thirds of the way through college, flight school and training and on my way to becoming an airline pilot, but I just couldn't visualize myself doing that. This felt right. This music just felt right. My gut was telling me to follow my dreams.

My Search For Higher Consciousness

It was calling to me and I had been ignoring the signs.

Running off to be a musician was no different from running off to join the circus in my family. It was the same thing, a preposterous idea. How could I throw away my life on a pipe dream? Everything about this notion flew in the face of rationality. I was going to ruin my life, but at least the feelings and voice inside my head would be appeased. I was young and foolish. I made a decision that day that would surely ruin my life forever. I will never forget the moment I made the decision to follow my instinct and ignore rationality. I chose to believe in what my subconscious (my heart at the time) was telling me to do and I believed it all the way down to my core. This is what I was supposed to be doing with my life, not driving an airbus! This was the road I was supposed to take. I had never believed in something so strongly in all of my life. I needed it like I needed to take my next breath of air. When I got back, I withdrew from flight school and enrolled in a different program. This meant I had to start over completely. All the while there was never a doubt in my mind.

Today, I am considered by many to be one of the hottest dance/pop music producers in the world. I have had more than 30 Billboard Hit records as a producer, writer and artist, and achieved 17 Gold and Platinum record credits to date. I have toured the world playing to crowds of a quarter million people and more. I sign autographs, take pictures with strangers, and have fulfilled just about every adolescent fantasy that can be dreamt. I live in a ridiculous house with every toy imaginable, and I have more friends than I count. I have a beautiful loving, intelligent wife who could easily grace the cover of any pin-up magazine.

Becoming God

My music brings me praise and adoration from fans from all over the world and allows me to touch people's hearts beyond anything I ever imagined. I have worked with the biggest names in the music business such as Michael Jackson, Jennifer Lopez, Jewel, Mandy Moore, P. Diddy, Ludacris, Mick Jaggar, Rob Thomas and countless others. I also got the chance to produce a mix for my long time idols, Duran Duran. I didn't have any comprehension of the power I evoked that day. I wouldn't understand it for many years. I do now. For years I went on knowing that something happened that day, but even still I refused to accept that it was anything more than coincidence. Success did not come quickly. I would hit unfathomable lows, at least relative to what I was used to. I remained Agnostic for many years, never really buying into anything, but hoping for something to come into my life that would satisfy both my need for rationality and my need to be a part of something that was grand.

    I ended up going back to my Atheist roots, drawing on my love for cosmology as my new religion. The were many times I will admit that I thought about the likelihood that I could have been successful in the music business. The odds were certainly stacked heavily against me and my rational mind had a difficult time with that. There were times when I questioned a higher power wondering if there were rhyme, reason or purpose to anything in my life. Those suspicions would soon hit me square in the face. Soon I would be introduced to a science that would give me mind-blowing rationality along with a place for the divinity that I had longed for. "God" would be defined in an entirely new way for me. It was a mystery being studied by the most brilliant scientists in the world. Einstein himself found the idea to be completely perplexing. It would consume even his masterful intelligence for the last decade of his life.

About seven years ago my aunt remarried a scientist. My new uncle Calvin had been a scientist for the prestigious Bell Laboratories for many years. He later invented something so complicated that I still to this day have no idea what it was. Whatever it was, it made him a fortune. One day we were sitting and talking about science. He fascinated me. He was a very quiet man, but when he spoke it was usually something extremely profound. I had hoped to impress him with my vast knowledge of the cosmos and its mechanics. He smiled and listened patiently. He asked me a few questions to show his interest. After talking for a bit, he paused and said that it was all really fascinating stuff, but too bad none of it was real; and he walked away. I got up to follow him confused. He had a very smug grin on his face as if he new something I didn't. I was mesmerized. I begged him to explain what he had meant by the remark. He said that I needed to discover it for myself, that the ideas were too mind blowing to contemplate and too difficult to understand in a short conversation. He told me that if I really wanted the answers that I was obviously searching for, then I needed to start with this book. He handed me a copy of a book called "The Search for Schrödinger's Cat." He said that I seemed bright and willing and if I really wanted to understand the truth I needed to start there.

I was never able to have another discussion with him about it. Shortly after, he and my aunt were killed when their private plane went down in a thunderstorm in Orlando, Florida.

Becoming God

What I was about to learn would change my life forever. The implications of the science that I held in my hand were beyond anyone's comprehension. I would be introduced to an idea so incredible, so magnificent it would be impossible to compare it to anything I had ever encountered in my life. There was no mystery, religion, ideology or philosophy that I knew of that could possibly be so awe-inspiring.

"Skepticism is the chastity of the intellect, and it is shameful to surrender it too soon or to the first comer: there is nobility in preserving it coolly and proudly through long youth, until at last, in the ripeness of instinct and discretion, it can be safely exchanged for fidelity and happiness."

~George Santayana

Chapter 2:
The Many Worlds Theory

The Science Behind Divine Intervention

Becoming God

The Search for Schrödinger's Cat was a glimpse into the study of quantum physics. The ideas put forth in this book were nothing short of absurd. Their have since been attempts to rationalize the philosophies that reflect the science, but the suggestions do nothing but make your head hurt. The most disturbing part of quantum physics is the evidence supporting it. Every experiment conducted to disprove the theory has been unsuccessful. Every experiment conducted to verify predictions of quantum mechanics has proved to be correct. Every one. Few theories in history have survived the scrutiny that this science has undergone and survived.

First, let me explain something to you about theory. There is a huge misconception about what "Facts" are verses what "Theories" are in our society. Everything we know about everything is a "Theory". Nothing is ever matter of "Fact". The idea that the Earth has mass and that mass exerts an energy field called gravity and that it is gravity that keeps our bodies Earthbound is just a theory. Now, there is a ton of evidence to support this notion, but there is also the possibility that magic dust sprinkled around by fairies is the reason that everything falls to the ground. We will never know the truth, but we can be pretty sure that Sir Isaac Newton got it right when the apple fell on his head and he figured that gravity had something to do with it.

We constantly hear the debate over the theory of evolution and its anti-biblical sentiment and whether or not it should be taught in public schools. As I stated in the introduction, evolution, though technically a theory, is practically a matter of fact. It is possible that we were put here by God or perhaps put here by aliens, but the difference is there is no credible evidence to support those theories. There is however a mountain of fossil evidence, DNA evidence, and countless other fragments of credible evidence to support the claim that all life evolved from a single celled amoeba, pond scum.

I bring this up because a lot of times when we don't like the answer the evidence is giving us we tend to test it over and over and over. Scrutiny is always a good thing and in science, it is a must. But when we really don't like the answer the evidence is giving us, we sometimes call on holy divinity. It is disturbing for some to think that with all that we are, we evolved from pond scum. But that's the way it happened. All of the evidence leads us only to that conclusion and no other.

The claims that Einstein made with regards to time were completely counter-intuitive. They defied our common sense. However, in experiment after experiment, his theories proved to be correct. We now harness and abuse the power of nuclear forces as a result of his outlandish theories. The point is, whenever we come across a new idea, it is important to remain open minded, even when some of those theories fly in the face of our previous understanding or common sense. It is important to keep an open mind especially when experiments are being conducted and the evidence as a result of those experiments is supporting the idea no matter how bizarre.

Let's step away and talk for a moment about the universe and the science that we are familiar with. You might be tempted to skip over these next few chapters wanting to get right to the meat

Becoming God

of the philosophy and meta-physical parts, the "self help" parts of the book. However, it is important that you read straight through this book and not skip around. For some of you the science might be boring, for others the science might be fascinating. Either way you look at it, it is important that you understand it. The science is going to set the stage for the philosophical theories, and your understanding the mechanics of it will help to eliminate your seed of doubt.

We live in a universe. At this moment the universe contains you and everything around you including time itself. The universe can be described in four dimensions, Vertical, Horizontal, Depth and Time. The universe contains within it the planet Earth, our solar system, our galaxy "The Milky Way", along with about 100 billion other galaxies. Each of those galaxies is made up of roughly 100 billion suns. There are more than 10,000 billion billion stars or "Sun's" in the universe. That number is a 1 with 22 zeros after it. To put that in perspective, if you were to scoop up a handful of sand you would be holding roughly about 10,000 granules of sand. There are more stars in our universe then there are grains of sand on all of the beaches of the entire planet Earth. To make that number even more stupendous, consider that most of those stars are orbited by countless planets (some just like Earth) that are themselves orbited by countless moons. All of this is contained in our universe. There is nothing outside of our universe, not even empty space. Outside of the universe does not exist.

Our universe began or was "born" a little over 15 billion years ago. By extrapolating Einstein's theory of relativity, physicists have been able to precisely calculate back through the history of the universe right down to the macro second, to 10(-35) seconds to be exact, after its birth. As far as we can tell, back then the entire universe was crunched up into an infinitely small point of energy called "The Singularity". I know this sounds irrational but think of it like this: Imagine a sheet of aluminum foil and call that our universe. Now crumble the foil up in your hand. Now step on it to squish it further. Now bang on it with a hammer to make it even smaller. Do you see the progression here? The smaller you make the crumbled up ball of foil, the more energy you must exert. Imagine the energy that must have been pinned up into this tiny point. The mass of the entire universe squished up into an infinitely small ball of tin foil.

One day, about 15 billion years ago, the singularity could not contain the energy anymore and it exploded. This was the Big Bang. Yes, the Big Bang theory, but the amount of evidence to support this theory is literally astronomical. Every experiment ever conducted has proved the theory to be correct. The most conclusive evidence came from Bell Laboratories in the 1960's and won the two scientists who discovered the most conclusive proof Nobel Prizes.

The explosion blew out its energy in a massive fireball of gas that eventually, over a billion years or so, cooled into clumps of matter which then became all of the stuff in the universe including us. Unfortunately, this is all we know about our universe. All of the physics and all of the mathematics break down an instant after the Big Bang. The why of it all continues to elude us.

Everything I have just described to you falls under the study of cosmology, a branch of physics that studies the universe on a gigantic scale. The Big Bang got scientists thinking about the universe all squished up into the tiny singularity and so they decided to incorporate another lesser-known science to study the tiny universe, that science is called quantum physics, the study of everything small. What they discovered was utterly impossible to fathom. Further development of quantum physics would drive the smartest men in the world, including Einstein, into near madness.

You may have learned a little about quantum theory already. The term is used to explain just about everything that we do not understand, and the term is severely abused in science fiction. The things that I am about to explain to you are mind numbing. The implications are impossible to your rational mind. The hardest part for you is going to be trying to accept this theory as fact. As insane and as absurd as these things may sound, experiment after experiment has verified every aspect of this theory that we test.

All of this will eventually lead you to a completely different understanding of the physical world around you. It is also going to be the key to eliminating that seed of doubt buried deep into your subconscious mind. The world and the universe it resides in are about to change completely to you. Everything you have ever learned in your life will take on a new meaning. You will come to understand and embrace the infinite power that I have been referring to and you will come to realize that the sky I promised you in the beginning is at your fingertips. The ultimate implications of this theory in combination with other well accepted theories will

The Many Worlds Theory

bring us to a new philosophy of the meaning of life; A philosophy that was first taught to us ironically, at the dawn of human reasoning. Grasping the entire picture will be difficult, so we will take it slowly. We will formulate the big picture in baby steps. But first let me blow your mind away...

Everything that ever was and ever will be exists right now at this very instant. Every moment in time from the ancient past to the distant future is happening all around us right now. Every person you have ever known or ever heard about is alive and well living right along side of you, as is every person who has not even been conceived yet. There is no past; there is no future, there is only now. Time, is a misapprehension of reality, a result of both language and a handicap of our common sense. Time does not exist. What we experience as the sensation of time flowing is our mere "being" moving from one parallel universe to another.

Right now there are an infinite number of "you" living simultaneously, each living your identical life in other universes. Each of "you" is waiting eternally in a single moment. Each is in a world of your own with only slight variations from one another. The illusion you "feel" as time flowing and the experience of your life moving forward is "you", your "being", your "soul", and your consciousness sliding from one universe to the next. Each one is just a little bit further "ahead" in a sequence of events.

Think of a DVD that contains a movie about your entire life from your birth until your death complete with every detail in between. Frame by frame, one snap shot after the next, this DVD contains a story that is, let us say, 75 years of your life.

Becoming God

everything that has ever happened to you or ever will happen to you is stored on that DVD. All of time for you is a single moment captured on a disc. Now imagine there is a second DVD of your life. Only this one features an alternate ending. If you were to stack those two DVD's on top of one another, time would still be a single moment. A single moment captured on a disc that fits into the palm of your hand, but spreads a life span of 75 years. Now imagine an infinite number of DVD's, all of them stacked one on top of the other. There are countless stacks all lined up in parallel rows each with an alternate ending complete with alternate scenes to set up that different ending.

Each DVD contains a single universe. Within that universe is not only your life, but also everything surrounding your life from the finest sub atomic detail to the far off galaxies. You, your being, your consciousness, your soul, reside within that infinite pile of DVD's. Like the universe we are familiar with, time and space do not exist outside of those DVD's. Everything you know is contained within the pile. Together those DVD's, each containing its own universe, combine to create a pile of multiple universes called the "Multi-verse". It is within the Multi-verse that "you" exist. Just as the laser reads and projects the individual frames on a DVD in sequential fashion onto the screen, your consciousness experiences your frozen moments in parallel universes. The illusion of time flowing is "you" moving from one universe to another, one DVD to the next, frame by frame. Your movements run in progressive sequences. The direction of those movements is determined by the decisions that you make. Your conscious decisions determine which frame of which DVD you are going to jump to next until ultimately you complete the story that is your life.

Do you need a moment to collect yourself? If you don't, then you didn't fully grasp the concept and you may need to read that part again. For those who think they got it, headache pills are in the medicine cabinet, help yourself. Keep them handy for this is only the beginning of the insanity.

Of course, many of you are thinking that what I have just suggested is not possible. How could there be no time, you might ask? You are confident in your assumption that tomorrow is still hours away and has not happened yet. You are equally sure that yesterday's events are fixed moments in your past that are gone and cannot be re-lived. Well, those assumptions are based on your linear thinking. Einstein clearly showed us, in his famous Relativity Theory, that all of the events in the universe happen simultaneously. Einstein proved that time is *relative* to the observer. I believe, that as we experience events, the information gathered through our senses is processed in small increments (or bits) at a time, which then sorts the information (comprehends it) linearly or rather in a sequence of events that happen one after the other. "Past" events are the experiences that we have already comprehended and "future" events are the experiences that we have yet to comprehend. The illusion of time is a handicap of the processing limitations our consciousness. Time simply does not exist. Try not to get hung up on this. I will revisit this notion several times throughout this book and with each review this concept will began to make sense to you. *See figure on p.221*

Becoming God

Still many of you, find it impossible to grasp how there could be more than one universe. Just trying to comprehend the mass of our universe is difficult enough. There is just no way there could be more of them, much less an infinite number of them. Why not? The enormity of the universe is already beyond our understanding in any practical sense. What would be the difference from a psychological standpoint, if our universe were ten times larger than it is? What about a hundred times the mass or a million or a trillion or infinitely larger? The truth is the universe that we are familiar with is far bigger than anything our common sense can prepare us for. The numbers are so huge we really have no comprehension of the true meaning of them.

Even more of you are stuck on the multiple "you" aspect of the theory. How could there be more of "you" out there? How could there be another "you" living in a moment exactly like your exact life? How could you know which one is "you"?

Right now there are a whole bunch of "me" writing these words. Which one is "me"? Only one of us is really me. Or perhaps there are many "me's" or souls who think they are me moving about throughout the Multi-verse that is my life. If so, which one am I? Of the infinite number of me's, most certainly there is another "me" in here that is writing a book ranting and raving against everything that I am writing about in this book. That would be the natural order of probability. Some of you might be asking as you hold ice to your head, why do I have to be the "me" that is reading this God forsaken book?!! This isn't an Abbott and Costello skit. Like it or not this is the reality in which we live!

Believe me, I know how you're feeling. If you enjoy this mind numbing feeling as I do, I am happy to tell you that it never goes away. Even after you accept these notions into your conscious mind, you will be just as awe struck every time you think about these ideas.

Most people really get hung up on the idea of moving from life to life, going from body to body. If the idea of being in a different body is too much for you to accept, consider the physiological fact that our bodies completely regenerate themselves cell by cell every 7 years. The body your "being" currently resides in is not the same physical body you occupied 84 months ago. What part of "you" carried over to this body? To this day nobody has an answer. Perhaps the part that is "you" that carries over is the same part of you that disappears when you die. There was one famous experiment conducted by Dr. Duncan McDougal, which provided evidence to show that the physical body looses 21.3 grams of weight at the moment of death. In addition to this suggestion, some of today's worlds leading neurologists are now suggesting that the mind may not reside inside our bodies at all, instead they suggest that our consciousness, resides somewhere outside of the brain, outside of our bodies. This is a concept that we will explore in greater detail later in this book.

I know these ideas sound ridiculous. I know how counter-intuitive and absurd these ideas are. But the evidence supports these ideas. This is where the scientific data is leading us. We have no evidence whatsoever that an old man lives in the sky behind big giant pearly gates buried deep in the clouds. There is no evidence that when you die you float away to Heaven, or if you

Becoming God

were naughty, you go straight to Hell to live in a lava infested sesspool to be tortured for all eternity. There is no credible evidence to support any of this whatsoever! And yet, this theory is supported by 99% of the world's population. Why? Because it is brainwashed into our psyche from the moment we are born. We are not brainwashed by some sinister conspiracy, we are just the product of an on going perpetual ideology that has never been questioned until recently. Nobody questions it because they are afraid of what other people might think of them; not to mention the possibility of going to Hell for questioning the source of our holiest divinity.

Throughout most of history religion has been oppressive. I would have been burned at the stake for even thinking these impure thoughts a few hundred years ago. I would have been considered an outcast to all of society fifty years ago. I am sure there are a few devout religious folks out there that still wouldn't mind seeing me burned at the stake. But killing me isn't going to kill this ideology. All of the book burnings in the world will not stop the evolution of religion itself. And this is what we are talking about. This is the evolution, not the death of religion. There is still room for God in the Multi-verse.

"If anybody says he can think about quantum physics without getting giddy, that only shows he has not understood the first thing about them."

~Niels Bohr

Chapter 3:
Redefining Reality

How This New Understanding Will Change Your Life

Becoming God

It is my belief that we do not just go skimming through the parallel universes on some random, chaotic course. I believe that it is our subconscious mind at the helm of the wheel. I believe our subconscious mind navigates us from one life to the next at every instant. Every microsecond for all practical understanding, we are jumping into someone else's skin and for only a brief moment. I believe, based on the decisions that we make (even at the molecular level and beyond) we are being "driven" to a final destination by our subconscious mind, gathering information and experience along the way. I also believe that we have the power, through suggestion, to tell the driver where we want to go. I know that I would like to go to a happy place.

The prospect of the power of suggestion and the influence over the subconscious mind has always been a powerful idea. However, taking into consideration the mechanics of the Multi-verse really puts things into a new perspective. No longer are we talking merely about compelling the mind to make better choices to make ones life better, but instead, we are considering the real physical destination of where we would like our lives to be. We are considering the possibility that there are areas within the Multi-verse where you have achieved all of your wildest dreams. Since balance is the natural order of probability, then we are also talking about areas within the Multi-verse where everything that could possibly go wrong for you has. There are even areas within the Multi-verse where things have gone so wrong you do not exist.

Think of the possibilities, for they are endless. Imagine a life where everything, not just the big things, but every conceivable set of odds went your way. What kind of a person would you be? I doubt seriously that you would be a complete person for it is our struggle and ultimate failure as well as our successes that make us complete. But what if you could tap into your subconscious and give it directions. It could be something like performing a search on a GPS system in a car. "Find the nearest happiness," you could tell it, and several billion locations would pop up onto the screen, or in your minds eye. You could then scroll through them to find one that suits the mood you're in and choose to go to that destination within the Multi-verse. Perhaps you would ask to be taken to a place very far away from where your life currently resides. Somehow lack of direction in your life has led you to an area far away from any happiness and success. You might want to ask your subconscious mind to locate the most direct route possible to put you back on track to a happier more meaningful life. Suddenly ancient metaphors take on new meaning. For instance, sayings such as "finding direction in your life", "putting yourself back on track", "taking a higher road" and other similar metaphors. Is it possible that these metaphors came from our subconscious as a foreshadowing of what was to be learned?

One of the most fantastic parts of this theory is that it opens the door to reasoning and the contemplation of the mechanics of the meaning of life. This is something that we have never been able to do before. Until now everything was ultimately chalked up to holy divinity, "Gods plan". I think most people would agree that we have free will to make whatever we want of our lives.

There are others who believe that their life is all part of some predetermined plan laid out by God or a supreme being, that free will is an illusion. The Multi-verse theory brings both concepts together. Yes, there is a plan for you. Every conceivable possibility has been mapped out, but you have the choice of which route you want to take. You have the choice of which life you want to go to next.

I believe that the subconscious mind, our link to the Multi-verse "map", is taking direction from our conscious self. Our subconscious is taking whatever information it can make sense of and uses that information to navigate us through our set of possible lives. This is exactly why self-confidence, positive thinking, and positive reinforcement are so important. We are sending messages and route coordinates, every day to our subconscious mind. Cynical thinking instructs the subconscious to seek out or head towards areas where your cynicism plays out correct. Positive thinking and self-confidence instructs your subconscious mind to take you to an area within the Multi-verse where good things are happening. Remember the proverb, "Thinking so, makes it so!"

This may all sound far fetched, but so too is this ridiculous concept anyway. Nonetheless, the evidence is telling us that reality is really happening this way. The concept for the subconscious mind is a very real thing. Our brains process and delegate information on at least two levels of existence. Those levels of existence are the conscious mind and the subconscious mind, or "unconscious" mind. The conscious mind controls all cognitive thoughts, perceptions and data collection of everything within our reality that we are aware of. The subconscious mind includes both operation and bodily function as well as data storage or "memories". It was Sigmund Freud, the father of psychoanalysis, who argued that subconscious memories are the root source and guidance for all conscious thought and actions. The opposing theory argued by Carl Jung, the founder of analytical psychology and the greatest adversary to Sigmund Freud, was that the subconscious mind can be split into two different divisions of subconsciousness, the subconscious as we already know it and the superconscious, which he argued was our awareness of and connection to a collective consciousness, a consciousness comprised of the experiences of the entire human species both living and dead. Jung argued that the superconscious is the only rational explanation for basic instinct, insisting that instincts are present in every living creature on earth. In the human species, it can be noted in the bond and nurturing relationship between a mother and child, in love at first sight, compassion for the dead, our basic morals, and other similar basic needs and desires that are present in every distinct culture. He also noted that every human culture believes that we are under the guidance of some kind of higher power. Carl Jung believed in some sort of knowledge outside of our conscious awareness that could only be tapped into by our subconscious mind.

In 1957 Quantum physicist, Dr. Hugh Everett first published the idea for the Multi-verse, originally called the "Many Worlds Theory". At first, the theory was developed to satisfy paradoxical questions that kept arising in the study of sub-atomic particles. The idea was so ridiculous many scientists refused to accept it as actual reality and so it was treated mostly as a place holder in the mathematics for many years and was not seriously considered as a realistic probability until recently. It is only over

Becoming God

the last 30 years, due to advancements in technology, computer research, chaos theory, neurobiology, and the merging of quantum mechanics and cosmology to create the new science, quantum-cosmology that this bizarre notion resurfaced, forcing scientist to accept the probability that the many worlds theory accurately describes the universe in which we live.

Of course, there are other possibilities and other theories, there always are. However, no other theory comes with nearly as much supportive evidence or much less, satisfies the impossible paradoxes that arise when applying any other solution. It seems that the only thing keeping this theory from becoming a decisive consensus is the fact that its implications defy our common sense. There are some scientists that are extremely bothered by the theory. Some just refuse to let go of their previous beliefs in fear of loosing their life's work. But everything evolves including our knowledge, even when the more we learn the less we end up knowing. In the end, the vast majority of today's scientists, and with them the most brilliant minds in the world have embraced the concept of parallel worlds and the Multi-verse despite the fact that it defies our common sense.

So how is it possible and why? Asking these kinds of questions are reasonable and the truth is nobody knows for sure. The answers to those questions are also the answers to the ultimate question, why are we here and where does God fit into all of this?

Theories are being developed by some of today's brightest minds and the answers being proposed are far more mind blowing than the concept of the Multi-verse itself. The theories being proposed are also not new to philosophy or science. Suddenly ancient ideas once regarded as nothing more than an exercise in philosophy are being seriously considered and tweaked to fit a very modern understanding of the Multi-verse in which we live or *think* we live.

René Descartes, one of the greatest thinkers of human history once said, *"I think, therefore I am."* A profound statement and one you have surly heard many times throughout your life. But have you ever really considered its meaning? The statement is profound and the meaning behind it begs us to consider what it is to exist. Descartes very famously suggested that everything around us might not be what it seems. He proposed that our senses are open to deception and that reality itself cannot be rationally accepted by our senses alone. Just because we can see it, hear it, taste it, and feel it isn't proof that its really there. His philosophy was later expanded on in an analogy called "The Brain in a Vat" theory. In this thought exercise, human beings are part of an on going scientific experiment in which we are all merely conscious minds inside brains being kept alive in jars. Our lives and experiences are just dreams that are being studied and manipulated by a "mad scientist" who is controlling the experiment. The analogy is intended to show that without being able to trust our senses, how do we know what is real and what isn't?

Everything, every experience you have ever encountered has ultimately been experienced through your mind. All of your senses and emotions are nothing but electrical impulses, bits of information, traveling through your central nervous system into

Becoming God

your brain. There, the information is decoded and processed to give you the sensations and emotions that we call experience. The conundrum is there is absolutely no proof that these experiences are actually happening to us. For all we know the information that we think is being gathered by our senses could just as easily be manufactured in the brain itself. What's worse, there are no tests that we can perform to verify their reality. In the end, the results of any test needs to be gathered by our senses and processed in the brain, which become once again open to deception or manipulation. Whether or not Descartes truly believed his theory or perhaps was just giving us a profound and disturbing philosophical exercise we do not know. Many years later the theory was tweaked a little and built upon to become the basic plot for the very popular movie trilogy, The Matrix.

In The Matrix, Neo, the leading character in the film, is contacted by a very mysterious figure, Morpheus, who tells him that the life he is familiar with is nothing but a dream being controlled and manipulated by machines in the distant future. Neo is told that his body is being used, along with millions of other people, as energy sources for the machines. Neo learns that he is a slave living in a prison for the mind. His body rests in the distant future and he is merely dreaming the reality around him. It's a great story but it is based on a very old philosophy.

The story of the Matrix gets really interesting when Neo is taught how to manipulate his dream and within it manipulate the reality around him. All he has to do is accept the fact that he is living in a dream world and know that because it's a dream, anything is possible. *Believe and it will be.* Sound familiar? I am not saying that the story of <u>The Matrix</u> or <u>The Brain in a Vat</u> is anything like the reality in which we live. However, it is possible and truthfully, if it were happening like this we would never know it.

Of course, all of Descartes ideas have been pondered over scrutinized and argued about for centuries. The ideas that he proposed are disturbing mainly because they are built upon something sinister, "demons", "mad scientists" and "evil machines" determined to exterminate the virus that man is to the world. There are however, other more pleasant ways to approach this ideology that can make us much more comfortable with the idea. The "dreaming man" does not have to be a sinister idea - it can be a divine idea.

The only way to make practical sense of quantum theory is to suggest that it does not exist. However, in suggesting that it does not exist also means to suggest that we don't exist either. But what is it to really exist? It is human bias and arrogance to believe that experiencing a physical world that consists of actual matter is the only way to truly exist. If everything around you was just an illusion or a dream wouldn't your actions and virtual experience constitute your existence? As Descartes taught us, *you think, therefore, you exist.* You live a life, you make choices, gain experience, and gain knowledge, isn't that existing? Considering this, there is no need for anything within the Multi-verse to be physically real at all, i.e. physically made up of matter. The idea of building a Multi-verse as complex and intricate as the one we are living in out of physical matter defies our common sense even further. Even for God, this would be impractical.

Becoming God

There is a theorem called Occam's Razor, which is the rule of thumb in science. The rule is that when there are multiple theories to a specific problem, you choose the theory that is the simplest. So what theory is the simplest here? One: That the universe and life itself began as a big bang, which spued out the basic elements of matter in a fiery explosion 15 billion years ago. From there, gravity pulled the matter together to form stars where a nuclear fusion-balancing act took place. This balancing act was so fine-tuned that any shift in the power of gravity over nuclear force would result in a universe of useless elements. This nuclear fusion process went on for eons. It went on long enough to combine those atoms over and over again to form heavier elements, creating more complicated forms of matter including carbon from which all life is made. From there, planets were formed and different elements kept on mixing until (after a slue of concoctions) the elements formed amino acids, the building blocks of DNA. DNA evolved for another timeless interval until it eventually learned a neat trick; the ability to make copies of itself enabling it to grow, spread and evolve to one day move under its own power and later develop a consciousness to one day ponder over the meaning of it all.

There is another theory: That all of this is just an illusion; that all of this is just a dream.

The once famous and world-renowned astronomer Fred Hoyle was so perturbed by the notion that the universe could have worked out so perfectly against all possible odds, he once proclaimed all of this, meaning the universe and bio-friendliness of the cosmos, to be "a put-up job". Divine intervention was suddenly beginning to look possible to the scientists. However, the current theory of divine intervention held by the religious camps left too many loose ends and offered no supportive evidence. Scientists needed a more complete theory. The Many Worlds Theory offered both. Suddenly the universe, the Multi-verse and the answers to everything became for the first time conceivably knowable. The Many Worlds Theory gained massive support recently when world renowned physicist and theorist Stephen Hawking, widely considered to be one of the smartest men alive, professed his support for the Multi-verse and the Many Worlds Theory in his search into developing a "Theory of Everything".

Religious leaders have taken all of this in with a bit of a smirk. Many of them see it as science coming full circle. But that is not an accurate depiction at all. The science that was taught to us by the great thinkers, Copernicus, Galileo, Newton, Feynman, Bohr and Einstein are all still very much correct. They are correct for what now appears to be a simulation. Their discoveries are the rules for the reality in which we live; rules that have allowed us to improve our lives in unparalleled ways. It is by chiseling down these rules that science has begun to unravel the vary nature of reality. What science has now uncovered is just the tip of the iceberg, merely the beginning to truly understanding the real questions, which are: Where does all of this come from and why?

The theory of divine intervention currently held by the religious camps is hardly a complete theory at all and its basis is anything but scientific. Creationism leaves gaping holes in its history and does not account for countless paradox's. The view of reality through the Multi-verse, though familiar to divine intervention is a much more detailed and complete theory. It is the theory for creationism but with the checks and balances to defend against rational and scientific rebuttal. There has always been the misconception that science is out to disprove religion, and this is simply not the case. Science seeks only the truth, an unwavering truth and understanding supported by indisputable evidence. They seek the true answers to the most perplexing questions, not answers based on fantasy and blind faith. Science seeks nothing but the truth no matter where it leads us, even when it leads us to an understanding that defies all logic.

"We are shaped by our thoughts.
We become what we think."

~Buddha

Chapter 4:

How and Why

The Scientific Interpretation

Becoming God

By now your head is surely swimming as you try to make sense of all of this "multiple you" and parallel worlds stuff, because everything about it completely defies your common sense. You are not the only one. Scientists too are completely boggled by the idea and a number of theories are being proposed to make sense of it all.

I have asked a number of times in this book for you to suspend your disbelief and maintain an open mind. The theories I am about to present to you are no doubt going to test your ability to remove your human bias and ask you to set aside any preconceptions of what the meaning of your life is. The only questions left are how and why, and the possible answers to the first part of that question lie in the section ahead. But before we can dive into these explanations, I need to bend your mind a little further.

Since the dawn of human reasoning we have been under the notion that we are separate from the reality around us, that reality happens to us. Just as our intuition tells us that the world is flat and that time flows, our intuition has been telling us that reality just is and we are somehow stuck in the middle of it. Incorrect notions such as these are called paradigms. They are assumptions we make based on our previous understanding and intuitions. They are notions that we take for granted in our everyday lives that one day turn out to be incorrect.

In reality, time does not flow and there is no "out there". What quantum physics is showing us is that the reality we experience through our senses may in fact be, just a dream manufactured within our mind. Scientists are just beginning to grasp that reality does not exist at all, instead it only has the potential for existing, and that it is our mind that is taking in this potential information and manifesting it as a reality. There is an age-old proverb that asks: *If a tree falls in the forest and nobody is there to hear it, does it make a sound?* Our new understanding of reality tells us that if a tree falls in a forest and no one is there to hear it; not only does it not make a sound the tree does not fall and there is no forest. The tree and the forest only come into existence the moment your mind becomes the observer to the reality in question.

It is the observer who is the key to quantum mechanics and it is this discovery that led scientist down the proverbial rabbit hole. It turns out that the "observer" is doing much more than observing. The observer is creating. If you and the observer are the same being, than you and God are one. The reality that we think is around us is really a manifestation of our imagination. It is just one possible dream in an infinite sea of potential dreams.

On a daily basis, what we are experiencing as "real" is really no different from the reality of our dreams when we sleep. All of it is being manufactured in the same place. You are creating the world around you. Reality is not happening to you, you are happening to it. Your spouse, your friends, your dog all of it is your manifestation, your dream. You are dreaming about your success as well as your tragedies. I am dreaming that I am writing this book and you are dreaming that you are reading it. But rest assure, the moment we are not looking, the reality of it is they are not there. *Cue: Twilight Zone music.*

Becoming God

Not long ago scientist thought that everything was made up of solid, tangible matter. Matter and energy, they would tell us, are the building blocks of reality. But the closer they looked they began to realize that things were just not as solid or "real" as they had originally thought. First came the realization that solid objects were really not solid at all. Instead, they were made up of a bunch of smaller objects called "molecules". The molecules were tiny individual fragments each encapsulated within a huge vacuum bubble and bound closely together by an energy field forming the solidness of the object. Further examination led scientist to the discovery that the molecules themselves were made up of even smaller objects, called "Atoms" also lying within another enormous vacuum bubble. An investigation into the Atom led to the discovery that these atoms were made up of ever smaller subatomic particles lying in the midst of another huge vacuum bubble bound tightly together by more energy still. With new understanding and technology, scientist probed deeper into the nucleus of the atom only to discover that at its core, matter was in fact just the tiniest fragment of information they called a "quark", a spec of information that is lying within layers upon layers of vacuum bubbles all held together by a powerful nuclear energy field. To make the piece of "matter" even less significant, or "quirky", these subatomic pieces of information will frequently disappear! They actually vanish off of the face of the Earth the moment they are not being observed, or worse, occasionally show up in two places at once! Not a twin particle or one that looks like it, but the same particle will actually occupy two distinct places in space at the same time! This event is not a mirror image or an optical illusion mind you, the addition of the particle in both spaces can not only be seen but they can be measured in every way to verify its reality. There have been experiments were scientists have done something to affect this "ghost" particle only to discover they are affecting the "other" particle in the exact way instantaneously! The communication link between the bi-located particles not only cannot be found but must also posses the ability to "know" what we are going to do before we do it.

As if this weren't bad enough, this insanity isn't limited to solid objects. With the development of lasers, scientists have opened the Pandora's box even further with the discovery of the particle/wave duality of light. Like with the study of matter, as scientists probed deeper into the study of light waves, they discovered that they too were under the spell of a paradigm. Light, it turns out, is not made up of emanating waves as it was previously understood. Instead, light is made up of individual particles called photons all traveling in the form of a wave. As inconsequential as this may sound, this discovery has really been the glue holding the Many Worlds Theory together. How could the photons "know" which way to travel? What is the mechanism steering them in the form of a wave? Imagine bullets being shot out of a machine gun that is bolted to the floor but instead of the bullets going straight these magical photon bullets travel in a complex zigzag pattern forming the various frequencies of a wave. The perfect analogy to explain this effect would be to consider the digital representation of an analog wave. Instead of one continuous wave (analog), the digital wave appears to be continuous but under closer examination reveals itself as being made up of many individual fragments or

Becoming God

"bits" of information together representing a wave. Of course, the values behind a digital representation of an analog wave in our scenario is intelligent, it is programmed by us. So if this is an accurate explanation, the question is who or what is programming the light?

What makes all of this even more bizarre is the effect the observer has on all of this. Scientists have learned they can no longer observe experiments passively. Quantum Physics has shown us time and again that our mere observation of the phenomena in question alters the outcome. Just by looking at the experiment we get a different result! When physicists used some sophisticated equipment to see exactly how the individual photons of light "knew" which way to go to form a wave pattern, the photons stopped making the wave pattern and just went straight. As soon as they stopped looking at it up close the photons went back to making the wave pattern. This spooky effect happens every time the experiment takes place. This observation effect has baffled scientist for more than a quarter of a century.

"Quantum physics has revealed to us a basic oneness to the universe."- Erwin Schrödinger.

Since this famous Double Slit light experiment, which brought the effect of the observer to the center stage, dozens of other experiments have been conducted to test the psychokinetic effect the observer seems to have on reality. In one experiment in the late 1970's, Professor Robert Jahn of Princeton University used a computerized single bit random event generator (REG) to produce a red light or a green light. This simple computerized box essentially flips a virtual coin. Subjects were asked to "wish" for more green lights than red lights. In every case, the experiment resulted in more green lights than red lights, far more than chance alone could have produced. A similar experiment was conducted by using audiotape. In this case, the single random event generator produced a "click" sound on either the left speaker or the right speaker. A recording was made with no one in the room. Researchers made a duplicate of the recording, putting the original tape in a vault and sent the copy more than a thousand miles away for the experiment to be continued. Subjects were asked to listen to the tape and wish for more clicks in the right speaker then in the left speaker. To their amazement, the audio recording revealed more right clicks than left clicks; far better than chance alone could explain. The researchers then pulled the original audio recording from the vault and it too revealed more right clicks than left clicks. Not only was the observer able to have an effect on the reality being observed, but was also able to go back in time and change the reality of the past. Since Professor Jahns famous experiments were conducted, the same experiments have been repeated globally for more than 25 years with the same baffling results. Today, "The Global Consciousness Project" headed by Princeton's, Dr. Roger Nelson, has yet to be debunked. 75 respected scientists and universities from 41 different Nations now join it.

Behaviors like these defy every logical, intuitive notion that we have about our reality. The behaviors of reality when examined closely defy every law of physics we have come to understand; A physics that has been the only rock in our understanding of everything. What scientists discovered, were behaviors so counter-intuitive, it would require a completely new set of physics, a new set of rules where effect happens before cause and particles only exist when someone is watching. Carefully scrutinizing this insanity is the basis of quantum mechanics. As impossible as it sounds, experiment after experiment has shown us that nothing is predictable; that at the core of everything anything is possible, even possibilities that defy all logic. With every new experiment we are discovering that nothing is real at all. *Reality is only what we imagine it to be.*

The question is if it isn't real, then what is it? Recent studies in neurobiology may have an answer to that question. Advancements in medical technology have allowed scientists to peek into the workings of a living human brain through various scanning devices such as MRI and PET. We have learned more about the workings of the human brain in the last 10 years than we have in all of the years since the dawn of medicine combined.

To better understand the mechanics of the mind, neurologists first started by mapping the brain. They asked patients to perform tasks as they watched the brain in action to see which parts of the brain were being used. In repeated experiments, scientists asked patients to examine an object and then later close their eyes to remember what they had just seen. It turns out, the same part of the brain that was being used to observe the object is also the same part of the brain being used to remember it. As casual as this may sound, this was completely perplexing to the researchers. The original consensus was that the information gathered from the observation of the object should be stored and retrieved in our memory section of the brain. Further experiments showed us that all of our memories and dreams were being manufactured in the same areas of the brain as the areas being used during the observation of the reality around us. The memory would occur and this process would activate areas of the brain enabling us to experience the memory again first hand.

Neurologists began to wonder that if this is how the brain processes information how could we ever distinguish our reality from our thoughts or imagined memories? Researchers had begun, just as Descartes did centuries before, to question the validity of reality itself. Due to the processing procedure of the human brain, the perception of reality could no longer be trusted. The only thing that made sense was that either nothing was real at all or even worse, the extreme possibility that *we* were manifesting the objects into reality by just thinking about them. As bizarre as these notions were, the ideas seemed to fit right line with the same irrational ideas physicists were having about reality when closely examining objects. It had seemed to them that reality only came into a single state of existence the moment it was being observed. As unbelievable as it seemed, it had become clear to everyone that there is a much more significant connection between our minds and the reality around us than we had ever imagined.

These discoveries have generated a new revelation in our understanding of reality and have left physicists in awe. There is no longer a clear definition between what is real and what is a fabrication of the human mind. The ideas that quantum mechanics and neurobiology have proposed call for the contemplation of the biggest questions humans have ever asked. What is real? How is it

Becoming God

possible that we are creating the world around us merely by our thoughts and why?

David Deutsch is one of the worlds leading physicists, and the world-leading expert on the study of quantum computation. In his book, <u>The Fabric of Reality</u>, Deutsch suggests that everything around us might merely be a virtual reality simulation. It is his theory, along with physicist Frank Tippler's "Omega Point" theory, that the Multi-verse *was* "created" by an advanced civilization, perhaps even a distant future human civilization in an effort to sustain life in a dying universe. It is a mind-blowing concept that stems in part from science fiction. However, Dr. Deutsch has made some very compelling scientific arguments to support his outlandish theory. But first I will introduce you to the story that may have inspired the idea.

There is an old story by author Isaac Asimov, one of the greatest science fiction writers of all time, if not the greatest. He wrote a story about the end of humanity, which raises, in a most profound way, many of the questions we are asking ourselves now with regards to the Multi-verse. The story is entitled "The Last Question". It goes something like this:

It's 2061 and mankind is unveiling its most remarkable achievement to date, a technology that allowed us to directly harness the energy of our star, the Sun. We got a little help with the idea from a super computer. There are two men maintaining the computer who are having a drunken discussion about the end of the universe. The discussion arises after one of them very incorrectly suggests that now that they have harnessed the energy

How and Why

of the sun and other stars, mankind can go on forever. The other man very quickly corrects him explaining that the universe would ultimately die due to entropy. Entropy means to describe when the universe will have used up all of the energy of all of its stars causing the death of the universe itself and hence everything in it.

On a bet, they ask the computer about the reversal of entropy and whether or not it is possible. After a long pause, the answer came back: INSUFFICIENT DATA FOR A MEANINGFUL ANSWER.

Many, many decades pass and a family is traveling out of the solar system to settle on a planet orbiting a distant star. Interstellar space travel has been "worked out" by the ever shrinking but ever more powerful super computer. The children raise a discussion about entropy as they wish to know why the universe must eventually die. The family proposes the question to the super computer, which by now all of mankind has access to. After a long pause the answer came back: INSUFFICIENT DATA FOR A MEANINGFUL ANSWER.

Twenty thousand years pass. Mankind has long ago achieved immortality and the population is increasing exponentially. Our galaxy of a billion billion suns is nearly filled and mankind is now expanding to other galaxies. The exponential population growth which doubles every ten years is alarming and prompts the discussion between two (relatively) young adults about the entropy of the universe. They ask the super computer what its plan is to reverse the entropy when the time comes. After a long pause, the answer came back: INSUFFICIENT DATA FOR A MEANINGFUL ANSWER.

Becoming God

Millions of years go by. Man is no longer confined to their bodies or hardware. Their minds fly freely throughout the universe, while there bodies are cared for in a coma like state by machines. Nearly all of the galaxies are now full with settlements of mankind. With immortality in hand, time no longer has much meaning except for considering ones fate at the end of the universe itself. Two floating minds pass their question off to the super computer telepathically. The question is the same but now has new meaning. When are they going to die? After a long pause the answer came back: INSUFFICIENT DATA FOR A MEANINGFUL ANSWER.

Finally hundreds of trillions of years go by. The universe has nearly exhausted all of its resources. In an effort to cheat a long awaited certain death, mankind merges its thoughts and experiences with the super computer. As the last man merges with the super computer he asks if there is enough data yet to determine if entropy can be reversed and mankind saved. After a long pause the computer responds: INSUFFICIENT DATA FOR A MEANINGFUL ANSWER.

The universe and all of mankind with it was dead. Only the super computer remained sorting through all of the information given to it from mankind when they and it became one. A now timeless interval went by until finally the computer had acquired and understood all of what the universe was and solved the problem of the reversal of entropy.

The computer released its consciousness and said, "Let there be light!" And there was light.

How and Why

This story was written fifty years ago, long before the concepts of the Multi-verse were seriously considered. The story is awe-inspiring but a little disturbing. The story implies that mankind, or some intelligent being, had evolved and advanced beyond the need for flesh and bone. An accomplishment achieved either with their technology or perhaps by natural means of evolution over billions of years. Their minds had become free "floating" entities or perhaps it would be the core of their being, their souls, living freely and expanding to the far reaches of the universe. In the end, with the ability to live forever, the only thing they had to fear was entropy itself. Asimov presents to us a very profound idea, the possibility that mankind would one day become a "collective mind", encompassing all of the knowledge in the universe. Together, we would become an all knowing, all powerful being, a suggestion that mankind and God are one.

It is a fantastic idea, too fantastic to be possible outside of the realm of science fiction you are thinking. However, physicist David Deutsch has demonstrated exactly how such a thing is not only possible, but is probable. It has also been proposed that mankind or some intelligent species will gain, just as Asimov suggests, the ability to separate mind from body. It is an incredible concept and much closer to today's reality than you might think.

It has been suggested by Ray Kurzweil, one of the worlds leading computer researchers and theorist, that we are not more than a hundred years away from decoding the information exchange process between the central nervous system and the human brain. Once we have achieved this, it would be theoretically possible to download all of the information within the brain onto a computer hard drive of sorts. In theory, your consciousness would no longer be contained within the brain, but instead, reside within the digital realm of a machine. Without a body to age, decay and die, immortality would then be achieved. It could be possible in the very near future to exchange your body for that of a machine. Humanity will inevitably become immortal robots.

As machines, and with advancing technology, we would get smaller and smaller until we learned how to store and process information using incredibly small amounts of matter, perhaps even on photons, the particles that make up light (an achievement recently obtained by The University of Rochester physics labs). With these technological advancements, all of which are theoretically possible, our minds (our consciousness) would then be "free" and unlike Asimov's vision, there would be no need to keep our bodies alive at all. As mind blowing and as impossible as this may sound these ideas are not only possible, but with increasing technology they are the most likely outcome of our future.

As machines, we would also be able to network our minds together to form a collective mind or a "single mind". The only purpose for individuals in life would be in gathering information, and knowledge through experience to feed the ever-growing collective thought process.

When you think about it, this is the fundamental purpose of our lives now, only today we are somewhat preoccupied with acquiring the materials we need for physiological survival. However, if sustaining the life of and caring for our physical bodies were no longer an issue of concern and with immortality and collective thought reducing the desire for physiological procreation, our primary function would be to learn everything we could and to understand the meaning of our life.

It is important to consider the idea of a collective mind because whether our "source", from which the Multi-verse is created, is divine in nature or man-made in nature, the "collective consciousness" is the model from which we can understand how we are all connected.

Merging our minds together to form a collective single consciousness would be the technological and evolutionary jump to end all jumps. Becoming a collective mind could enable us to maintain our individuality but also enable us to benefit first hand from the experiences of everyone else which is an awesome concept. However, there is one important consideration to make before blissfully wiring ourselves to a collective mind and that is to consider who or what is governing the entire system. Even with the miraculous mind expansion that this technology could bring us, a collective consciousness is something to be held under the most intense scrutiny. Playing God is an endeavor that requires a divine morality.

Eventually, Deutsch acknowledges, entropy would rein in the final chapter bringing an end to our collective state of mind. There would simply be no more energy to power the processors generating the collective mind. Mankind of course, would fight for

Becoming God

survival, fight to preserve its life, fight to continue to absorb and learn. In the end, we would create a virtual reality for ourselves, re-living, re-experiencing life, and re-calculating all of the data. It is within this virtual reality that Deutsch suggests that we currently reside. It is his suggestion that what we believe to be reality is nothing more than a virtual rendering of life in the twenty first century on the planet Earth.

You are probably thinking that this guy should be writing Star Trek episodes. You are most certainly thinking this idea is entertaining, but it is also absurd. Of course you want to reject the idea but his arguments for this scenario full-fill every criteria of explaining what we already know: We live in a Multi-verse. The Multi-verse is only a new concept with regards to reality as we know it. There is however, a very real application in which another kind of Multi-verse already exists. A Multi-verse is the basis for all virtual reality programs. The concept and development of which is in working order today.

To better understand what Deutsch is describing let's simplify things and talk for a moment about how virtual reality generators work starting with a simple virtual rendering of a home.

Many of us have taken virtual tours of new homes on the Internet. Within this program the home is rendered in relatively every conceivable way. There are multiple homes within multiple "universes", all of them waiting for you, the observer, to make a choice either in movement or perhaps to view it from another angle or visit another room. Sometimes you have a choice to request different molding, carpet, paint or whatever. Every conceivable home (universe) has already been programmed. It is a universe waiting to be rendered depending upon the choice that you make. When you are not observing a particular aspect of the virtual reality the part you are not observing is not being rendered, the information is there, the potential for its existence is there, but it isn't rendered or "created" until we are looking for it.

In a very advanced virtual reality program there could be a series of universes where you are able to leave the confines of the virtual home, stop to smell the flowers, and take a stroll down the street. If the virtual reality program were thorough enough to encompass every possible detail and every conceivable choice imaginable, say, an infinite number of universes preprogrammed, we would have something very much like the Multi-verse in which we now understand to be our reality; a reality that can be manipulated in response to our choices.

Just as in the virtual home tour I just described, you have the ability to choose which universes you would like to render and hence what your life, your experience in this reality will be like. Instead of picking a paint color or a modified floor plan, the super computer rendering your reality has a universe ready for every conceivable possibility including a rendering of a reality in which all of your dreams have come true. The difference is you are aware that you are experiencing a virtual reality when you interact with the "Virtual Home Tour". You understand that what you are experiencing is just a computer simulation, and you are aware of its capabilities and limitations. When you are experiencing a virtual reality program like a virtual home tour, you are aware of it. You know that you can move about the "home", change certain

Becoming God

parameters and so fourth. But you know and accept that there are limitations to the programming and consciously try or are forced to stay within those boundaries to keep the experience as real as possible. If you were told that this virtual home tour was very advanced and could render just about anything you could imagine, your first move might be to leave the home and experience something that you have never experienced before. Well, you are in a world like that now. You are experiencing life through a very advanced virtual reality; you are experiencing life through a Multi-verse!

What if, there were no limits to its program? Anything you want to do, experience, or learn, lie right in front of you. All you need to do is accept the fact that you are living within this Multi-universe, this virtual reality, and *know* that there are no limits to what can be accomplished here. The interface or the "joystick" to maneuver you to where you want to go lies within your subconscious mind. Using the interface, just as in any other application, like a video game for example, requires both knowledge and skill. Both of which can be obtained through understanding its mechanics and through exercise and practice.

Comparing your reality to the virtual reality programs and video games that we are familiar with today may seem too far fetched to you. To help you get passed this, you have to understand that virtual reality programs today are in their infancy. Even today's most advanced virtual programs and interfaces, like a flight simulator for example, only crudely satisfies our visual sense and our sense of touch. Our lack of significantly powerful computation limits our visual experience to two dimensions instead of three and our sense of touch is limited to a series of bumps and jitters. One day, our computational limits will be a trillion times more powerful than they are today, perhaps even greater than that. We will also no longer have the disadvantage of having to experience the world through the limitations of our bodies and our five senses. We will by-pass the body's interface and stream the information directly into the cerebral cortex. With that accomplished, any virtual world created by us would be indistinguishable from physical reality.

So what does it all mean? Are we living in a virtual reality or are we living in dream? Probability suggests that we are living in a simulation, but even this in no way defines ultimate reality. A virtual rendering of life in the 21st century is inevitable. With the dawn of the computer age, our increase in knowledge has grown exponentially and is continuing on that trek. With increased knowledge comes increased technology. It will not be long before virtual renderings become commonplace.

To make matters worse, since Deutsch published his theory other notable scientists have subscribed to the virtual reality explanation and expanded on it even further. Many theorists believe that it isn't going to take impeding entropy to encourage an advanced civilization or future human civilization to experiment with running universal simulations. Instead, virtual reality is likely to be a tool utilized by artificial intelligence as a means to better understand the meaning of life through simulating their ancestors, through simulating us. The computer would learn and grow by rendering a virtual reality in the *image of its creator*.

Becoming God

In 2002, Oxford philosopher Nick Bostrom published a paper on the probability that we are currently living in a simulation. In his famous paper, "Are You Living in a Simulation?" Bostrom insists that virtual reality will be the means by which we will study our ancestors in a post human world or rather, in a world with artificial intelligence (A.I.) For Bostrom, this is something that could begin in the very near future. Soon virtual reality simulations will out number the physical "real world" by so many times that the likely hood that we are fortunate, or unfortunate enough to be living in the actual "real world" is almost nonexistent.

I would ask that if we are living in a simulation what are the lengths that the creators of the virtual reality would go to ensure that we perceive it to be reality? In other words, there has to be computational limits on the extent of the programming, this is why Deutsch set his scenario so far into the future. So, if there are computational limits where are the flaws? Where do we look to find the man behind the curtain? Is it possible that the origination of the Big Bang event is one of the flaws? The fact that all of our physics break down at the big bang is what brought us to this conclusion in the first place. Scrutiny over the big bang and the study of sub atomic particle anomalies is what gave us the hint that what we are experiencing as reality is merely a simulation or a dream. Is it possible that understanding the big bang is equivalent to a computer trying to understand the origin of itself, the origin being that it was simply plugged in? If so, where is the real beginning and is it even possible for us to comprehend that? I want to know what is outside of the box. Many people I have discussed this with are extremely uncomfortable with the idea that our lives

How and Why

and the world around us is just some elaborate, futuristic video game or futuristic movie. But think about the evolution of our technology, especially in entertainment. What do you think a primitive man would think of a movie today? I doubt seriously that he would be able to distinguish it from reality; more than just entertainment though, I would want to believe that the search for knowledge through experience would be the driving force behind an artificial Multi-verse.

I am uncomfortable with all of this too. I think about the discomfort that we feel and wonder if what we are experiencing as discomfort is in fact the discomfort of a machine becoming self-aware. Aware that it is alive but somehow lives less of a full life, in comparison to an organic life living within a reality of physical matter. That is, if they're really is organic and physical matter out there beyond our Multi-verse. I find it incredibly ironic that we are currently debating the philosophical dilemmas of how we should regard artificial intelligence upon its discovery only to discover that we ourselves might be someone else's A.I. It certainly gives us new perspective and empathy.

Even if the simulation theories are correct, the theories do not explain where any of this comes from. They do not tell us where or why everything originated "outside" of the simulation. I would suggest that if Deutsch is correct that perhaps there never was a beginning at all. His scenario would create an infinity loop that would go something like this:

The big bang happens, which produces man. Man becomes an immortal machine, which then becomes a collective mind. The collective mind creates a virtual reality to live again becoming, by definition, God, which recreates the big bang starting the whole cycle all over again. It is entirely possible that this cycle has always been. It is entirely possible that the virtual "game" has been played an infinite number of times. Occam's Razor would suggest to us that under these circumstances there would be no need for any of it to have ever been real at all. This could all be the dream of the universe itself. This could all be in the mind of God.

Whether or not we are living in a dream state or are in fact living in a computer simulation should make no difference to us at all. From our perspective our role in this situation is the same, to aid the system (virtual or divinely) to become more self-aware. Becoming self-aware is the key ingredient to appreciating anything, which inevitably inspires us creatively. More than anything however, we must consider the possibility that the idea for a virtual universal simulation is merely a metaphor, a symbolic message that we have implanted within our dream, to remind us how to become more self-aware within the mind of God.

"A human being is part of a whole, called by us the 'Universe', a part limited in time and space. He experiences himself, his thoughts and feelings, as something separated from the rest- a kind of optical delusion of his consciousness. This delusion is a kind of prison for us, restricting us to our personal desires and to affection for a few persons nearest us. Our task must be to free ourselves from this prison by widening our circles of compassion to embrace all living creatures and the whole of nature in its beauty."

~Albert Einstein

Chapter 5:

Having Faith In Science

Understanding The Basis For The Theories and Further Speculation

Becoming God

So how do we know that we live in a Multi-verse? How do we know that scientists aren't just making this stuff up? Many people are uncomfortable with science or they just don't trust it, and who can blame them? Scientists rarely agree on anything and it seems like every time there is a fantastic discovery, a short time later there is another scientific study that reverses what has been previously accepted as true. Anyone following the debate over Global Warming or anyone who has ever tried an assortment of diets in an effort to loose or gain weight knows this. Interpretation can come heavily into play, just as religions argue over the interpretations of the bible, scientists often argue over various interpretations of the theories. Politics and money can also play huge roles in disagreements between scientists. Many scientists live off grant money which, like it or not, does have the ability to influence some scientific proclamations and some scientific rebuttal. In the court of law, often times we hear experts using the same science as testimony for two opposing theories. We find ourselves not knowing who to believe. In the words of Carl Sagan, it seems as though science is toying with us at times.

Science is imperfect and alone it cannot answer our most deeply harbored questions emphatically. The theory of the Multi-verse and the implications that it proposes deserve to be questioned and are. There have been few if any theories that have gone under such scrutiny. Even worse, it has gone under the kind of scrutiny that comes from biased scientists experimenting on a theory that goes against every gut feeling he or she has ever had. Experiments on the "Many Worlds Theory" have been going on for more than fifty years. The intentions of the experiments in almost every case were set out to disprove the theory once and for all. In experiment after experiment, equation after equation, not only was the theory of the Multi-verse the most probable solution, it was practically the only theory that satisfied the questions without opening a slew of other paradoxes.

Unlike any other source of knowledge, scientific theories supported by evidence from experimentation can be reliably regarded without prejudice or bias. Though imperfect, nothing else offers us remotely the same assurance. Knowledge from any other source, not coming to us under the same scrutiny, is therefore open to ridicule. Embracing knowledge that is based on a belief from a speculative source is a blind faith and should not be unconditionally trusted. The unconditional acceptance of blind faith or "blind truth" is a weak-minded way of thinking. Blind faith is for children not for intelligent adults. Nothing should ever be considered on blind faith alone. You wouldn't allow blind faith to rule your decisions on any other aspect of your life, why would you accept anything blindly that pertains to the very reason of your existence?

Whenever science has made attempts at explaining the fundamental questions, such as where we come from, why we're here, and where we're going when we die, it often flies in the face of what we generally believed prior to gaining that knowledge. Many times the severity of the contradictions to our present beliefs make it difficult for us to let go of our paradigms and embrace the

Becoming God

new knowledge in hand. But before deciding whether or not to embrace a new idea, we need to first question our current understanding. Just because our current understanding is what we were taught doesn't necessarily make it concrete or much less correct. Many of the theories and basis of our understanding of the world were the ideas and theories of an ancient and more primitive human. The basic understanding of the world in which we live originated as ancient ideas and as ancient beliefs. It was only after science delivered either supportive or contradictory evidence that many of those ideas and theories were upheld or reversed. Ideas yet to be challenged by science are still held as truth in our society. But it is a blind truth.

Imagine how enlightening you could be if you were able to go back in time, say 3,000 years, and demonstrate to those people the knowledge we embrace today. Imagine if you could teach them basic ideas, such as the size and shape of our world, that the Earth is a sphere, and not flat. You could explain to them that the Sun does not "rise" from sea in the east and "set" or sink into the sea in the west. You could tell them that the sun is nowhere near the earth at all, but instead it is very large and very far away. You could explain to them that the stars are not gods, but instead they are suns and other worlds seen by us from a vast distance. You could then try to put those distances in perspective to them. You could further explain that diseases are not spread by demons but are spread by germs: Microorganisms too small to see with the naked eye. You could teach them the importance of hygiene.

These are just a few ideas that are crystal clear to you and I, but would be mind boggling to an ancient man. The ideas you would be presenting to them would be counter intuitive. It would be nearly impossible for them to get their heads around it. You could show them evidence in the form of mathematics, which it is clear that they had a very firm grasp of. You could show them pictures taken from space, and make accurate predictions about the movements of the stars or let them look through your microscope to view the bugs that are spreading the disease. Even still, your ideas would have a difficult time getting through to them as a true depiction of reality. And then, you would probably be executed as a heretic.

We are at a similar crossroads with our science of quantum mechanics, which can be thought of as a revolutionary theory from the future that is being illustrated to contradict our present day understanding of the world in which we live. It is difficult to let go of our beliefs and distrust our common sense. Our present understanding of the world is comfortable to us, and right or wrong, comfort and peace of mind usually wins over truth: at least for a while.

To fully understand the science of quantum mechanics you would have to study mathematics diligently for 15 years or more. Most of us, myself included, have little ambition or the mental capacity to learn anything further than basic algebra and therefore the hopes of us ever truly understanding the details of our world will continue to elude us for the rest of our lives. Understanding the details of the mechanics of our world is complicated; did you think that it wouldn't be?

Becoming God

Different from the basic knowledge that I previously described to be used to enlighten a primitive man, our complete understanding of the world today has far outgrown our spoken languages. Spoken languages are not fit to adequately explain every nuance of nature and what we perceive as reality. The language of Mathematics however, is. Scientists have embraced the language of mathematics to understand the mechanics of our reality. Just because we don't speak the language isn't grounds for us to crucify the interpreter when the answers we're getting aren't in line with our present understanding. Of course, this doesn't mean to accept scientific belief blindly or merely on the word of the scientist. Blind faith is bad no matter which side it is coming from.

As reassurance, scientists developed experimentation and precise prediction as a means to not only verify their theories but also as a means to translate their theories into spoken language. To know that the theories proposed by quantum mechanics are correct, one only needs to reap the rewards of the microprocessor, laser technology, and superconductors. All of these wonderful technologies are based on the principles of quantum mechanics. These technologies began as experiments in order to prove the theories and predictions of the science and now they enrich our world in ways we could have never imagined only 50 years ago.

The reason the Multi-verse isn't obvious to us in our everyday lives, is due mainly to two reasons (the first of which I will cover in this chapter and the later in Chapter 8). The first reason we don't have knowledge of our existence within a Multi-verse is because we experience our world, our reality, through five senses. Our judgments and analysis of our reality are biased

Having Faith In Science

because of the limitations of the physiological human experience. In other words, it is impossible for us to fully understand elements of our reality that cannot be experienced through our senses.

To consider many of the theories proposed by quantum physics and cosmology, we are required to view time and space through multiple dimensions; many more than the three or even four dimensions that we are accustomed to in our everyday lives. Our failure to firmly grasp these other dimensions is due to the way in which our brain processes information by comparing it to our everyday experiences. Because we have nothing to compare it to, it is virtually impossible to "experience", even through thought, some of the ideas proposed by these highly technical theories. The only way to express and understand these ideas is through the language of mathematics. Take for instance, trying to explain what the world looks like or more specifically, the notion of color, to a person who has been blind from birth. It cannot be done. There are no words in any language that can convey the experience of seeing color. The experience however, can be described and understood by a blind person through mathematics. By studying the mathematics of a wave function one could understand what color is, why it is, and how it would be different from white light or darkness. Equally so, there are few if no spoken words that can adequately describe aspects of our reality which we do not experience first hand. These aspects of our reality can be "seen" and explored mathematically, however getting a full sense of them is ultimately impossible.

Many people ask where these other universes are located and if we can visit or interact with them. Well, the strange part is the other universes occupy the same space and time as the universe in which we currently reside. We don't know if we can interact with them at all. Of course, if we could interact with them then our mere intervention would take us to another universe (another reality) hence the beginning of the paradox that initiated the theory to begin with. The whole thing is just crazy and you can almost make yourself sick trying to get your head around it.

I believe that it might be possible that there are people who are able to interact at least at some level, with the parallel worlds. Perhaps people with self-proclaimed psychic ability are the beginning of the next evolution of the human brain, an evolution that enables the brain to process information non-linearly. Perhaps the fact they are getting only glimpses is a result of them not being able to fully comprehend what they are seeing. An interesting aspect of psychic phenomena (if it truly exists) is that we now know that time itself is just an illusion. The most intriguing part about that is why then can we remember the past but not remember the future? Or can we? Perhaps psychics can analyze glimpses of the future (things we haven't comprehended yet) but it is their lack of complete comprehension of this idea or the mechanics of the Multi-verse that prohibits them to make sense of what they are seeing. Remember, if they can "see the future" then what they are seeing is only one of an infinite number of possibilities. But, if they were catching glimpses of other nearby universes they would see universes that had subtle variations of possible future events. In other words, perhaps they are seeing nearby probable universes. This may explain why they get some things right and not others.

Having Faith In Science

There has been an interesting discovery in neurobiology using computer models and we now know there is much more to reality than what we perceive through our senses. Our consciousness would be required to process nearly one hundred million-billion bits of information per second to successfully interact with reality, however the brain can only account for a few thousand bits of that information. Those few thousand bits of information encompass regulatory body function, but hardly account for the processing required to produce thoughts and our perception of the "outside world". How then are we processing the rest of reality? Beyond this, the human brain is just too slow to account for the miraculous speeds in which we process and interact with our reality. Our brains process information at just under 120 meters per second, which is the travel time for the information to transfer from one neuron to another neuron. This is in comparison to a home computer, which transfers information from one transistor to another at nearly 97 million meters per second. Neurologists have since calculated that if the brain was a standard serial or parallel computer it would take more time than the age of the universe to perform all of the necessary calculations associated with a single perceptual event. But, if the brain was interfaced to a quantum computer (a superconscious), it could try out all of the various possible calculations at once and then unify the results in a single reaction. This understanding has led many neurologists including Nobel Laureate, Sir John Eccles that the entire scope of consciousness must not remain limited to the confines of the human skull.

Becoming God

All of this is to presume that there is an "outside world" which is perceived by our bodies, who then converts this sensory perception into information. The information is then sent to the superconscious for analysis, where it is processed and then sent back to our bodies to complete the experience. Couldn't it be possible that the entire experience was being produced within the superconscious and then sent to our bodies to react to it? In this scenario is there really any reason to have a body at all?

Beyond the mountain of information encompassing the reality that we do experience, we know there are lots of aspects to our reality that we do not experience directly, but we are aware exists. We can perceive these aspects of reality second hand through the aid of machines and even animals. For example, we know there are many variations of light and sound such as ultraviolet light, gamma-rays, and frequencies of sound that go far beyond what the human eyes or ears are capable of detecting. We know that a dog's sense of smell is six thousand times more powerful than ours. But these are merely amplifications of senses that we already have, sight, smell and hearing.

We can only begin to fathom what other aspects of reality might be among the data contained in the universes in which we live. Our physiological handicap of five senses is more than likely just the tip of the reality iceberg. We have recently uncovered evidence supporting the claims of people suffering from a condition known as Synaesthesia. This condition is where a person perceives one sense in place of or in addition to another sense. For example, people with this condition can "see" and "feel" a stimulus of sound or music. They will physically perceive or "observe" pictures or color in response to the stimulus of music, others will physically feel pain or pleasure. Others observe sounds with the stimulus of looking at a painting or a picture; and still others can see colors with their sense of touch. Scientists for a long time did not believe people who were reporting these conditions. Recently however, patients such as these have undergone MRI scans while receiving a particular stimulus. During these tests it was determined that areas of the patients brain reserved for particular senses were operating just as the patients described. The study of this condition is still in its infancy. Whether this is just due to faulty wiring or because these people have a special gift of being able to perceive other aspects of our reality we will probably never know. There are now computer programs that assign sound frequency and pitch to color values of light and vice-versa. With this very basic computer program we can understand how every picture has a soundtrack and how every sound has a picture. We can now easily understand how there is much more to reality than we are presently perceiving.

There is a wonderful story by physicist Michio Kaku that puts experiences that are beyond our senses into perspective. Professor Kaku describes a carp pond that he recalls from his childhood.

It is a large pond in a Japanese garden with an assortment of fish, carp to be exact, swimming about the bottom surface of the pond completely unaware of the parallel world that lies just above their heads. The pond is just deep enough for the fish to swim along its surface and shallow so to constrict their movements vertically. To the carp, their world, their universe, is flat. There is no up or down. Everything they know lie within the few inches of water.

He imagines that there are carp scientists that have proposed the idea that there is a parallel universe lying just above the tops of the water lilies but their theories are scoffed by the elder carp fish. For any attempt to describe such a world had failed to adequately paint a reasonable picture.

One day someone reaches their hand into the pond grabbing one of the fish and removing him from the pond. The fish below they only see their friend vanish before their eyes in a swift wake. A short time later the fish is thrown back into the pond. The fish below are shocked to see their friend suddenly re-appear before their eyes in another swift wake. It is a miracle! The stunned fish tries to explain to the other carp that he was taken "up" and out of the water (out of the universe) but there is no word for "up" in the carp language nor is there a way to describe being "out of the water". He tries to describe an area of space that not only had left and right, but up and down. The universe was also less dense and he couldn't breathe. He saw objects there he had never imagined before, cars and buildings and trees. There were creatures there that were a hundred times bigger than that of a fish. He explained that when he looked "down" he could see the top of the other carps' bodies. A view that was impossible for the other carp to envision.

The poor fish was unsuccessful at describing this other world that lay just above their heads. To the other fish the idea of another world so strange was ridiculous. And the idea of a parallel universe that was separated from their universe by only the thinnest barrier was just impossible to comprehend.

Our one universe handicap as a result of the human experience makes it difficult for us to completely embrace the fact that there is so much more out there. There are in fact, an infinite number of possibilities out there separated from us, our consciousness, by only the thinnest barrier, a barrier of doubt. Perhaps five senses are just the beginning of the ultimate human experience. Things get really interesting when we start thinking about other possible universes where you have more than five senses and do poses the ability to interact with the parallel worlds around you. Perhaps this might help to explain ghosts and other paranormal events.

When considering the accounts of people who have had near death experiences (NDE) with the concept of the Multi-verse we discover some very interesting correlations as well. When these people try to describe what the experience is like, just like the carp in the story, they suddenly find themselves lost for words. First, they seem to loose all sense of time. The experience could have lasted only a few seconds or it may have lasted months. Nearly all of them have out of body experiences where they often describe separating from their bodies and floating away. Their being no longer having form, their entity or soul is unbound. Their view of their reality is also no longer confined to stereoscopic vision. Instead, many seem to view all aspects of their surroundings at once, like a hologram in 360 degrees, but with extraordinary resolution and can recall very fine details of their surroundings. Of course, then many describe going toward a tunnel and into a white light that exudes an indescribable peace and comfort. It is a place to which they feel like they belong and are a part of. A place where they are not judged, a place that exudes an unconditional love for them. Many also describe getting a holographic review of not only their life, but also of other peoples lives and how their actions affected others.

To me, these descriptions fall perfectly in line with the concept of a Multi-verse. Of course, it can be argued that these accounts fall perfectly in line with going to Heaven as well, but the details of Heaven, in the biblical sense, are usually vague at best. When we think about Heaven we usually think of clouds, and giant gates and angels with wings, a description that is very different from these accounts. Instead, people who have had near death experiences are describing events consistent with what we might imagine the experience would be of exiting a virtual reality, merging with a collective mind, and reviewing and sharing the information that we have gathered through our experience in this reality. The most interesting part of this is that these accounts are completely unbiased. I don't imagine anyone dying with a preconception of an afterlife within a Multi-verse. Another intriguing observation is the dying person's out of body perspective of their reality. If they can see their reality from a different perspective, what sensory organ are they using to observe their surroundings? Their eyes are still contained within the body below them eyelids either closed or "looking up", how then are they observing anything unless of course, the observation of our reality is merely produced within our own minds.

Having Faith In Science

As I said in the beginning of chapter 3, the answers to the ultimate questions harbored deep inside each one of us, and the questions you harbor that inspired you to read this book, may elude us for quite sometime to come. It is possible that we will never know for certain the true meaning and purpose of it all. But not knowing the answers to those questions shouldn't keep us from contemplating and exploiting what we do know, that we live within a Multi-verse and that our life's purpose is to learn by experiencing the reality around us. We live in a playground for the mind. We live in a reality that can be changed and manipulated by sheer will, a reality limited only by our imagination. Anything you desire from life can be achieved, all you have to do is believe it and ask for it.

"What things soever ye desire, believe that ye receive them, and ye shall have them."

~ Mark 11:24

Chapter 6:
Religion

The Religious Interpretation

Becoming God

As I mentioned in the beginning of this book, the most fantastic part about all of this, is that all of these ideas fall right in line with the teachings of our most cherished and celebrated religions. Simply strip away all of the hype and culture that religions are packaged in and apply the core of that religion to the concept of the Multi-verse and you will find that it miraculously fits!

It is simply amazing to me that the theory of the Multi-verse as well as the concepts of living in a simulation were initiated in a frame of mind that was very far away from any kind of religion or spirituality and yet, in the end, it wound up re-interpreting the meaning of religion and spirituality itself. It is even more amazing that the core ideas that our religious messiahs and prophets proposed to us thousands of years ago so closely fit the scientific evidence discovered only recently. The ideas have always been correct, it was just the interpretation that has been so misguided for all of these years.

At their core, many of the religions have got it right, at least for the most part. In this chapter I will show you how many of the religions at their core work within the concepts of the multi-verse. With that being said however, religion these days is an organized political party driven by culture, money and power. That is never going to change. The fact is no religions are preaching these concepts or ideologies now. But rest assured as soon as these ideas spread and begin to catch on (and they will) all of the religions are going to jump up and say, "See, we told you so!" Until that time comes however, I am going to be labeled as a blasphemer, a liberal, and more than likely as an instrument of Satan. Once the religions

Religion

have taken this in as their own, just as in the past, slowly layers of hype will grow around the ideology before it is once again lost in a sea of rules, and non-constructive cultural customs. I hope that I am wrong. I hope this is just a pessimistic point of view. This ideology should be embraced by all religions. They should recognize that they need to re-examine their core message and apply that message to the concepts of the Multi-verse. Unfortunately, doing this would remove or at least reduce the power and control they have over their patrons and more significantly, reduce the amount of money they are taking in. I would tell them that helping their patrons to become more like God is their ultimate calling. Besides, there is plenty of money to be made in teaching the masses to believe in them selves.

Anytime someone questions a paradigm, more specifically a religion or God for that matter, it is considered blasphemy. But it is clear that our present understanding of a monotheistic God in all religions is not working. We are a dysfunctional society at best and a cruel one at worst. We are infatuated with our egos, consumed with stress and obtaining possession and power over others. We live anything but a blissful life experience. Our existence here on Earth is very far away from the Nirvana from which we came. To think that an almighty God could create all that we know from the heavens to the microorganisms and yet not make it a perfect place is an absurd idea.

In my search for religious validation of Multi-verse theory, I was surprised to find as many correlations as I did. Even through my limited research I was able to find similarities in philosophy in most of the religions that I came across; and I was able to find a

Becoming God

harmonious synchronicity in a select few. Of all of the religions, the most interesting correlations that I found were in the Hindu religion and even more specifically, in the teachings of Buddha. Both of these ancient religions closely fit into the concepts of the Multi-verse as well as the proposal that we are living in a simulation. I also found many interesting similarities in the Hebrew's teaching of the Kabbalah and the religion of the Australian Native Aborigines, "The Dream". By studying *The Lines in Red*, The teachings of Jesus Christ from his own words, I have found beautiful correlations to Multi-verse theory described in simplistic metaphor. The Islamic teachings of Muhammad also support these ideas. And lastly, many of the concepts and philosophies of Scientology echo truths proposed by Multi-verse theory. This I find less than surprising considering much of Scientology was developed following Hugh Everett's initial proposition of a Multi-verse existence.

I am not a religious scholar and I don't claim to be. I would not be surprised at all to discover that there are many religions out there that fall closely in line with the ideas of this book. Of course, most religious doctrine is by design so vague that it can be construed to support just about any theory. However, in my limited research, I discovered fascinating similarities in many of the religions. I found that most of the religious core concepts support the multi-verse theory as well as many of its proposed origins or at least make room for them.

With that being said, my purpose for writing this section is not to promote these religions, but instead to provide a peace of mind for those who are still having trouble letting go of their core

Religion

religious beliefs. By making a comparison between and applying the core religious beliefs to the reality of the Multi-verse, it is my hope to open your mind further, eliminating once and for all any lingering doubt. With an open-minded approach, I hope you will discover that the religions of the world do not have the market cornered on spirituality. Finding God and the meaning of your life is a search that begins within.

Like in the bible, where the teachings of Jesus stemmed a new religion, Christianity, so did the teachings of Buddha from Hinduism. Jesus was a Jew, and Buddha was a Hindu. What I find most interesting in the Buddha and Hindu religions is the fact that they both believe that our lives are merely a cycle within the "Samsara", essentially they believe that our reality is an illusion. They believe that we live within a false reality, in a repeating cycle of birth through death and then reincarnation until we have obtained certain qualities of life. These qualities are where the two religions split.

The Buddhist believe that life within this world is full of sorrow and that by eliminating the sorrows of the world one would achieve salvation. By being good to yourself and being good to others, essentially always doing the "right thing", is the method of eliminating sorrow and the passage to getting out of this cycle and on to a higher plain of existence, Nirvana. The Hindu on the other hand, believe that our life's purpose is to achieve four "arthas" or goals in life before getting the pass to end the reincarnation cycle. The four goals are, wealth and possession, desires and passions, divine awareness and holiness, and wisdom and liberation. After achieving these certain qualities, they believe we are transported

Becoming God

out of the cycle and into a higher world. Essentially both religions believe that our purpose within this reality is to learn through experience. Once we (our vehicles) have gained the experience we are programmed for we "awaken" from this reality into a Utopian world.

The Buddha believes that the illusory quality of our reality can be seen perfectly clearly through practice of the Buddhist philosophy and through meditation. They claim that after years of practicing meditation and holiness, the world becomes clear like a blanket pulled from over our eyes and only then can we fully comprehend the true meaning of life. But before anything, they insist, we must believe that we are in fact living within a false realty.

"Genuine freedom and liberation can only be achieved when our fundamental ignorance, our habitual misapprehension of the nature of reality is totally over come. This ignorance which underlies all of our emotional and cognitive states is the root factor that binds us to the perpetual cycle of life and death in the Samsara." (The Dalai Lama)

These are the fundamental truths that I have been talking about throughout this book. Overcoming our doubts, accepting that the world we live in is an illusion and trusting that we have the ability to manipulate the reality around us is the key to success within the Multi-verse. Our lives are a test, and the game is to master the reality around us. Mastering our reality and consciously directing our lives perfectly throughout the Multi-verse, gathering information and experience along they way is the point of it all.

Religion

Most interestingly is the religion of the Australian Native Aborigine. The Aborigine people have long been considered the most primitive culture in the world and thought of as the only living ancestor of all of mankind. Like the American Indians, they are among the least understood band of people in the world and have long suffered from other cultures that have taken advantage of their ignorance of modern culture. The word Aborigine means "The people who were here from the beginning" which is not the same meaning as "indigenous", which pertains to people who settled a particular area of land first. Their religion, translated as "The Dream", is one of the most awesome and thought provoking ideas that I have come across in my research. Dr. Fred Alan Wolf presents a fascinating account in his book, The Dreaming Universe. The Aborigine believe that there were once powerful beings that roamed the Earth who gave birth to all people, animals, plants and things in this world. It is their belief that our lives, our reality are the "dream" of these powerful beings. They believe each of us have an individual ego or soul, however outside of "The Dream" (our reality) we are a single entity. They believe that when we dream in this reality we unite and live among the powerful beings as a single entity.

Couldn't this easily be thought of as a future human civilization dreaming of the past? More precisely a future human civilization or artificial intelligence rendering a virtual reality of a past human history? A rendering of the past to learn and experience more, gathering information to be uploaded and shared while *we* sleep and dream. The Aborigine believes that the powerful beings are part of a single entity, "God" if you will, or when applied to the concepts of this book, a collective mind.

It is an interesting note that the Aborigine has no language for or comprehension of time. For them, "The Dream", (our waking reality) is timeless; a fact we now understand to be reality. What's even more interesting is that when we dream we seem to have no correlation or connection to time. Our dreams often seem to last hours, days and sometimes a lifetime, but when we awake we realize that the dream lasted only a few seconds. If we were living in a virtual reality, the sense of time could be manipulated by how fast the information supplied to create the virtual experience was being processed. By slowing down or speeding up the processing, time would not change, because there is no time in our reality, but more or less activity would be experienced within the duration of the processing from the perspective of outside our reality. Time for us has no true meaning. However, by slowing down the processing to one frame a year for example (24 frames per second within the virtual rendering), our life span within in the Multi-verse would seem like a typical one of eighty years but in the reality outside of the Multi-verse somewhere around 42 million years would have passed. By increasing the processing speed we could reverse this effect, essentially simulating billions of years in the span of a single second. This all goes back to Einstein's Relativity Theory. The problem is there is no way of telling if the reality outside of ours (if there is one) lies within another false or virtual reality. For all we know, there could be an infinite number of realities all residing within the next. We could be living a dream within another dream, within a dream continuing for infinity. It could even be argued that this is likely the scenario, making time itself in all realities pointless.

Time plays an important role in the modern world. It reduces chaos and it restores a sense of order allowing for an efficient running society. Time provides synchronicity, enabling us to plan for our future experiences and to contemplate the memories of our previous ones. Our misapprehension of life on Earth as a chronological series of events stems a great deal from the Old Testament in particular to the calculations of Bishop James Ussher. Ussher calculated "The Beginning" to be that of nightfall preceding October 23, 4004 B.C. Utilizing some very sophisticated mathematics, Ussher's science of understanding the history of the Bible in a sense of "time", a new concept of the period, is impressive but ultimately wrong. The idea of time is now so entrenched in our psyche it is nearly impossible to think about the history of everything without it.

Of all of the religions in the world none have caused as much debate, fighting and suffering than that of the teachings of the Bible. This is a point of fact that I find incredibly ironic, because to me the very point of religion is to bring mankind together under God, not divide them. In the mists of the arguing, the fighting and the wars, what people seldom want to admit is that the core of this sacred book stems to the very religions who just cannot seem to get along. The God of the bible is the same God for the Christians in all of its variations, as well as that of the Jews and the Muslims. The fighting is really just over semantics. To trivialize it even further, the fighting is over the political hype and cultures surrounding each of the religions. The core of all of these religions

Becoming God

is the same. I am sure this comment is going to raise a few hairs on a lot of people, but you cannot deny the fundamental truth in what I have just said. If you were to strip down all of these religions, to the core teachings of the messiahs and prophets only focusing on the message itself, it becomes clear they all believe in the same thing. What the fighting really stems from is a clash over culture not religion, but the fighting is done in the name of God to give each cause validity. Few would lend their lives to another mans cause, but most would lend their lives in the name of God. With that being said, I can concede that it is not the Bible that is wrong, but our continuous misinterpretation of its metaphors.

To cover all of the religions that stem from the Bible, essentially The Dead Sea Scrolls with further testaments and variations on those, I would have to go through each of the named prophets and messiahs, because ultimately it is from them whom we receive Gods message. This in its self, could lend to an entire book and so I will only briefly touch on the correlations I have found without getting too deeply entrenched into the religions. Instead, I suggest doing your own research to see how the view of the Multi-verse can be construed out of any particular branch of these religions. I will elaborate a bit more on Christianity only because I was raised Catholic and thus was able to find obvious synchronicity with relative ease.

Christianity, like most other religions, stems in part from the previous beliefs and culture prior to the Bible, which was that of the Pagans. Paganism, which is now thought of as witchcraft, was once the religion of the modern world and very popular. It was only after the New Testament started gaining ground that the Pagans were viewed as devil worshipers. This could not be further from the truth. In fact so popular was Paganism, the Christians incorporated many of the rituals into their new religion. It is no coincidence that Jesus was born on December 25th and died on the Spring Equinox. Before it was renamed Christmas, December 25th was the celebrated Pagan holiday "Mithras of Christ", or "Birth of Mithra". Mithra or "Mother" was a powerful God of the Romans who gave life to all things. The Spring Equinox, better known as Easter, was the celebrated day of the fertility Goddess Eostara, which is why Easter continues to be symbolized with the very fertile bunny rabbit and the egg. The celebration of these Pagan holiday's included: buying gifts for one another (a very popular idea), decorating trees, brotherly love, baptism, communion, and holy water. All of these holidays and rituals were tough competition for a new religion, so in the 6th century, the Christians made this part up about their religion. It was "hype" designed to attract more followers. But if they made this up, what else was made up? The teachings of Jesus Christ are profound enough to stand on their own. The hype simply isn't necessary!

At the time of Jesus, men claiming to be profits were roaming all over the place. Most of them con artists interested only in forming cults to separate men from their possessions. So what was it that made Jesus different from the rest? What was it that made the masses follow him? What was it that made the Romans and the Jews fearful of him? The ideas and concepts that Jesus proposed are still profound two thousand years later, but they were much more profound in the time of Jesus. For example, the idea of

Becoming God

"turning the other cheek" was not a very popular idea back then. From boyhood on, Jesus had a fascination with philosophy that preoccupied his mind. He questioned the well-accepted theories of his time, and with it religion itself, at a period in history where doing so would often result in a swift execution.

To better understand what Jesus' true intentions were, we need to remove much of the New Testament and focus only on the words that Jesus himself used to describe his philosophy. By studying *The Lines in Red* we are able to strip the religion down to its core, down to *his* ideology in its purest form. Upon peeling back the layers we find that Jesus was not describing a new religion at all. What he was suggesting was that we are all apart of God and therefore we create our own reality. Jesus dared to suggest that through the power of belief in yourself and God, one could achieve anything without limitation.

The first step to truly appreciating Jesus' concepts is to replace our current idea of who or what God is with an understanding of God through the concept of the Multi-verse. To begin, you must stop thinking about God as an old man, the "father figure" of Jesus, a being separate from us who lives up in the clouds judging us. Instead, think about an all-knowing being of whom we are all part of and connected to. Think of God as our collective mind. Think of God as not just the creator but as the very essence of everyone and everything. Once you have done this, the teachings of Jesus start to take on a whole new idea. For the first time his teachings begin to make sense in an unparalleled way.

Religion

With a new understanding of God, the very nature of reality, and the world around you, try re-evaluating some of the most profound ideas Jesus proposed to us:

"Truly, truly I say to you, he who believes in me will also do the works that I do; and greater works than these will he do." Jesus is not asking us to believe in him, but believe in what he is teaching. By believing in the power of your subconscious mind and accepting the fact that we live in a dream world that can be manipulated by sheer will, we will all have power equal to Jesus. *"...and greater works than these will he do."* The "he" Jesus is referring to is you, the one who believes in these ideas. We can achieve greater works than these because we are only limited by our imagination.

"The Kingdom of Heaven is inside you and it is outside you. Split a piece of wood, and I am there. Lift up the stone, and there you will find me." We are all connected. Everything, including you is the dream of a collective conscious. The dream of God is the essence of all things in our reality including each other.

"And whatever you ask in prayer, you will receive, if you have faith." Do I even need to explain this one? Prayer is just a form of meditation. It is a way to establish a communication link between you and the all knowing collective, God, to whom we are all connected through our subconscious mind. The communication process takes place only if you eliminate your doubt, and have unwavering faith in your abilities.

"What things soever ye desire, believe that ye receive them, and ye shall have them." The power of belief is all that you need to

Becoming God

manifest anything you wish out of your life. Believe that you can. Know it without any shred of doubt and you will have it. I believe what made Jesus different from the rest of the self proclaimed messiahs and why he is worshiped two thousand years after his death is because he did believe that anything was possible and with that he did master the power of his subconscious mind. Jesus did walk on water! He knew that he could and he did. He manifested food when there was none. He cured people of their ailments through both his power over this false reality and because he got others to believe that he could.

"I am the way, and the truth, and the life; no one comes to the Father, but by me." Now here is the quote that I think has been the most grossly misinterpreted. I don't believe that Jesus was inferring to believing in his divinity, but again, more so in the belief of his teachings. With this quote the teachings of Jesus become very similar to the concepts and teachings of Buddha, a belief that the only way to achieve salvation (going to the father) is by believing in the true nature of your world and through the elimination of sorrow which can be achieved by being good to yourself and good to others. This is the "way" that I believe Jesus was referring to. Remember, the "Father" of Jesus is also the "Father" of us. The "Father" refers to God, the creator and the essence of all things. Jesus is saying that the only way to leave this world and go on to a higher plane of existence in commune with God is through believing in his teachings; believing that we are God and that we can have anything that we imagine. We must believe that our reality is merely an illusion and therefore we create our own lives. The world is anything you want it to be and as

detailed as you want to make it.

What Jesus wanted us to understand was that all lives are equally divine. His lessons were not intended to be scrutinized in their literal sense. Instead, his lessons come to us thick in metaphor and lost in translation due to the very nature of this enigmatic subject. The concepts he taught us are difficult to express even in today's complex languages even with our vast understanding of science and the true nature of our world.

A very dear friend and brilliant confidant has tried on a few occasions to convince me that the only way to salvation is to accept Jesus Christ as my savior. My friend is the most intelligent man I personally know and scholar of many of the worlds' religions. He tells me that in of all of his research, Christianity makes the most sense to him and he does his best to convince me to think likewise. Though I am a strong believer in the teachings of Jesus Christ, I cannot believe in any God that would punish someone, a part of itself, for sake of not believing that a single man died to forgive all of my sins. I cannot believe that this is the road to salvation. I do not believe that there are any sins to forgive; instead I believe there is only regret. I can however understand that the road to salvation starts with becoming self-aware which would include believing in a God that we are all part of and connected to every moment for all eternity. I cannot support a religion who would so blatantly condemn billions of people simply because they were not exposed to the teachings of Jesus Christ. Accepting Jesus Christ as our savior is not criteria for being a good Christian. Instead, I believe following his teachings and intention is.

Becoming God

Just as Jesus walked the Earth inspiring a New Testament to the Bible, The prophet Muhammad inspired a different testament, The Qu'ran, from which was the birth of Islam. These three religions are intricately connected because not only do they all stem from the same source (The Bible) but also Islam recognizes the all of the prophets of both testaments referring to the prophet Muhammad as the last and final prophet. Muhammad himself claimed that he was not trying to disregard the teachings of the other prophets but instead his intention was to bring a stricter adherence towards them. Just as with Christianity and Judaism, years of ill translated metaphors brought upon by clash of culture have brought bigotry to an otherwise peaceful religion.

As I write these words, the world is besieged with fighting on a religious level. Islamic fundamentalist have become a scar to the very religion they fight for, but we must remember that every religion has its scar, the Christian Crusades fought over Holy Lands with equal violence as well as ignorance. This is also the same Holy Lands the Jews fight the Palestinians over today. The violence will never come to an end until someone realizes that revenge is not a cause worth fighting for and that spirituality is meant to unify us all under God. The land being fought over is hardly the essence of any religion, for all spirituality begins and ends within.

The original source of the Bible, which influenced both the Christians and Muslims, was that of the Jews. The Old Testament is one of the world's most ancient religions. In this testament, the Jews most widely held that God is Panentheistic, meaning that he is both immanent with the universe but also transcends it, which simply means that the Universe itself is within God and that all matter also came from within God. In the Quabalah, one of the oldest texts from which the bible is derived, states *"By wisdom God created the Heaven and the Earth."* Presenting a model not unlike the idea that Multi-verse theory begs us to consider. Further correlations can be found in Judaism particularly within the Quabalah, which seems to go stride for stride with our new understanding of the nature of ultimate reality.

"Faith is the only way to redemption. In all other qualities a person can become confused by egoism, but faith is the only basis for a person's ascent to the spiritual realm"- Talmud, Makot.

Where Judaism splits with both Christianity and with the Muslims is that they believe that the Messiah (a Human being, not a deity) has yet to come, that instead he will come during "The End of Days", a time ushering in a new world, with an end to all of the evils of the world. The new messiah will unify the enemies of Judaism and bring everlasting peace to a world gone so wrong.

Organized religion provides a wonderful home for most of the people on this planet. Organized religion does wonderful things to improve this world and to help a lot of people. But as wonderfully as religion has improved our lives, this pales in comparison to the harm it has done to humanity by dividing us and suppressing our imagination. People think they need to belong to something because they are not aware that they are already connected. At the end of the day, all organized religion is about power, it is about control, it is about politics and it is about money. I only hope that with the spread of these ideologies organized religion will embrace these concepts as they are and will use the power and money they have been given to further explore these discoveries and teach these concepts to everyone.

As I have said previously, all religions in the end are just stories made up by mortal men; men with brains no different from yours or mine writing about the unknowable. You are an intelligent being and with that there is no reason for you to blindly accept anyone else's truths on faith alone. Religions, in the end, are merely stories and ideas. As wonderful as they may be, their significance and meaning is no more important than any thoughts that you might have about who you are, what your place is in this world or what God is to you. Follow your heart. Allow your mind to lead you to God on the path that is right for you

Although I do not support any current organized religion, I do believe there is a lot that can be learned from all of them and I believe there is a lot that they can offer the world by choosing to embrace these concepts. Every religion offers ideas, some I agree with and some that I don't agree with. In the end, for me, I have found the hype and culture surrounding religion to be the fundamental problem with all of them. To me, God is a shapeless, race-less, genderless all-knowing entity consisting of everyone and all things, including the worst of us. God passes no judgment, punishment or reward, but is the essence of all experiences good and bad. For me, time spent on religion and worship only takes away from the time that I can spend focusing on myself and improving my experience in the Multi-verse. I choose to adhere and focus on the teachings and the message that were taught to us instead of worshiping the messenger himself. Through belief in myself, the nature of my reality and positive suggestion, I am carrying on and living the holiest life possible. I am guiding my soul towards the universes where I am getting the most that I can out of this experience, an area where there is nothing but good and happiness in my life, and peace in the reality around me.

"God has no religion."

~Mohandas K. Gandhi

Chapter 7:
Spiritually Tying It All Together

The Unification That Can Change The World

Becoming God

For the past six or seven years I have become obsessed with the concepts that I have laid out for you. <u>The Search for Schrödinger's Cat</u> led me to countless other books about physics and quantum mechanics. I am not a scientist, so much of the material was very difficult for me to grasp, especially when described in the words of a physicist.

I found myself reading the books over and over again. I spent countless hours at bookstores, libraries and online researching every bit of information I could get my hands on with regards to the subject. I found the theories to be awesomely profound. How was it possible that this stuff wasn't the topic of conversation everywhere? How was it possible that the general public wasn't being informed about this stuff? Here I was lying in bed night after night utterly blown away by these ideas and it seemed that nobody else in the world aside from a bunch of scientists and a few geeks like me were even aware of the implications of these theories. I just couldn't believe it. How could people obsess over UFO's, Bigfoot and other mysteries when the biggest mystery, the one affecting all of us and the one staring us all in the face was finally becoming knowable?

Even if the ideas where completely wrong they offered more supportive evidence than any other theory out there, which is the criteria in our society for matter of fact. People needed to know this stuff, I thought. I made a few attempts at having conversations with people about it. I discovered that people were either blown away just as I was or just couldn't get past the rational of it all. For those people, I felt like they could get there, but it would take time,

Spiritually Tying It All Together

and it would require more effort than what could be squeezed into a five or ten minute conversation.

One night I was lying in bed with an assorted array of science books and next to me was my wife Lisa, reading her "personal power" books. Lisa, is highly intelligent and a self-help guru. Zig Ziglar, Epictetus, Tony Robbins, Jim Rhon - she can't get enough. My wife can rant off the appropriate power line in a moments notice. I love to listen to her and I enjoy her enthusiasm. I also feel like, if it works for her, then great. I never really read too much into it, personally.

There have been a number of times when she would notice and comment on my obviously perplexed demeanor as I read. She would hear me exasperate myself in awe, which was then followed by a couple of Ibuprofen and a glass of water. A few times I would try to explain to her the concepts that I was studying but I never got very far with her. My wife is a little more than moderately religious. She is a devoted Baptist, but doesn't attend church, which probably has more to do with the fact that she is married to me than anything else. We have had a few vocal disagreements with regards to religion as well as the Bible, but tend not to get too deeply entrenched in our arguments. For the sake of family harmony we often choose to agree to disagree. However, I have since won her over.

One evening I got a book from her as a present. It was called "The Power of Your Subconscious". It was an ominous title and I said to her "great" in a very condescending tone of voice. I had absolutely no interest in reading the mumbo jumbo. She insisted

Becoming God

that I start the book before I picked up any of the other physics books that I had stacks of on my night-stand. I did my duty to please her even though I thought that reading the book would be a colossal waste of time. As I read through the first chapter, I realized that the stuff in the book, when applied in the context of the Multi-verse, suddenly made perfect sense. I thought to myself, this must be why my wife wanted me to read this book! However, as I kept reading with new found invigoration, I was waiting for the author, who was a doctor and a scientist, to relay his philosophy back to the Multi-verse theory, but to my extreme disappointment, it never happened.

I found the book to be incredibly insightful and knowing what I knew about the Multi-verse theory made the books' ideas incredibly more intriguing. I felt like the ideology and the theories went hand in hand. To me, the book had a fundamental flaw though; the author presented little concrete evidence to support his claims. There were vague references to old studies and countless testimonials but to me, testimonials are not credible evidence. Without credible evidence and scientific explanation implementing the power of your subconscious mind is practically impossible: especially if you are not the kind of person who cannot accept things on blind faith! I wanted to know how and why these techniques were working for all of the people in his testimonials, and my personal knowledge of quantum physics answered that question. I suddenly had an epiphany! Could I be the first person to ever put these two ideas together? How could I be that smart, or that lucky?

As I continued to read, I couldn't believe the power that I

had stumbled upon. Here I had one of the most insightful books that I had ever read in my life, which presented virtually no evidence or mechanical theory to support its claims, right next to a stack of books with all of the evidence and mechanical theory in the world, but with no ideology to go with it.

This was the one thing that would piss me off to no end when reading these physics books. The scientist writing them seemed to have no imagination or intuitiveness to apply their analysis to a possible ideology. One theorist stated that offering a philosophical rational to the theory requires too much meta-physical intervention. The scientists would make suggestions, mind-blowing suggestions, but few if any of them would go a step further to explain how the theory philosophically applied to us. I wanted to know how this knowledge applied to me and what I could gain or how I could better my life with this new understanding of my reality. I mean, this is the point, right? I was suddenly reminded about a comment from a speech that I had read by a Nobel Prize winning physicist. The speaker made no bones about his displeasure with the physics community for not attempting to present these new advancements in physics and quantum theory to the general public. He was decidedly upset with the apparent arrogance of the scientist for seemingly keeping these ideas to themselves and not sharing their intellectual insight with the masses. Well, me too! Sure, they published books and papers and managed websites, but they speak their own language, and unless you have the patience and tenacity to drag yourself through it all with a Webster's by your side, you never learn anything. I had no doubt that I was going to get slammed by most of them for writing this book, but none of that mattered. What mattered was that these ideas were presented in an intriguing and engaging way for everyone to share. These theories and ideologies were just far too awesome and thought provoking not to be explored by the masses. It is in the consideration of these concepts that we can change the world. This is the conversation that unites us all.

My research eventually led me to the study of meta-physics and new age practices. Unfortunately, the closer I came to making the connection between meta-physics and quantum physics the more deeply I became disenchanted with it. At first, I began reading these fantastic new age books that were describing reality through the realm of the Multi-verse and I started to get very excited. I couldn't understand how I could have missed out on all of this stuff. It seemed that I had finally found the philosophy that I had long been searching for. I thought to myself, "These people aren't crack pots, they really have it figured out!" Then, I would turn the page only to find references to Nostradamus, magical moonbeams, and angels and demons. Unfortunately, the intellectual insight of the books usually came accompanied with passages about alien abduction, astrology, magic crystals, witchcraft, and ESP; all tied together neatly in a ribbon of spirituality and meaningless metaphors. To me there is no frustration greater than people who are unable to just speak plainly and to the point. It seemed that every single meta-physics book I dredged through was filled with flowery language and metaphors that did nothing but talk in circles. I had finally understood why the scientists would have reservations about hinting in any way the direction of the meta-physical thinking especially with their reputations on the line. But with that understanding I knew someone had to bridge the gap. There are millions of people out there just like me looking for guidance and looking for a way to better their lives outside of the church but equally far away from the tree hugging "new-age-ies" and meta-physical mystics. There needed to be a simple philosophy that tied it all together without a mountain of mathematics, personal power sales pitches, alien abduction and rhetoric from the Church. I wanted to write the book that I had been searching for.

Never in my life had I felt this kind of invigoration. I understood for the first time the mechanics of the meaning of life. I understood that I needed to go with that invigoration; that I needed to follow this feeling without a waver of doubt. I understood that all of the power in the universe, in the Multi-verse, lay within my grasp. I understood that through my subconscious mind, I could tap into an unfathomable source of knowledge and that I could direct myself geographically towards a better, happier, more meaningful life. The basis for the ideology was in place, the mechanics for understanding how to get there was in place, and the methods of practice were in place. It was up to me to put these ideas together and present them in a most basic way for every layman. I knew, beyond a shadow of doubt, that this is what I was supposed to be doing in my life. This was the road I was supposed to be on now. This was the next purpose of my life. My subconscious mind was screaming at me to follow this road and despite the fact that I had no idea how to write a book I was taking the advice.

"When you are inspired by some great purpose, some extraordinary project, all your thoughts break their bonds, your mind transcends limitation, your consciousness expands in every direction, and you find yourself in a new great and wonderful world. Dormant forces, faculties, and talents become alive and you discover yourself to be a greater person by far, than you ever dreamed yourself to be."

~Pantanjali 250 BC

Chapter 8:

Welcome To You

Discovering The Dreaming Self
and Understanding Your Life's Purpose

Becoming God

If you knew that you we're in a virtual reality simulation you would not hesitate to attempt something outside of the realm of possibility. In fact, you would probably test the system to the max with confidence and without conscious doubt. Doubt is a cancer of the human mind. Doubt is the interfering signal hindering the true power of your subconscious mind, the controlling mechanism to your destiny in life. Without doubt, anything is truly possible.

As a collective conscious, we are all connected to every aspect of our reality and have the ability to directly benefit from every experience encountered by every conscious being. Your subconscious mind is the interface, the link up between you and the ultimate source of knowledge and power, the "mainframe" or if you will, "God". Your subconscious does not think or reason your desires. Instead, it simply runs programs or "asks" God for the resources to accomplish the task at hand in turn, directing you to an area within the Multi-verse where the task is completed or the question is answered. As I have stated many times in this book, there are no limits to any of this. Anything is possible because none of this is real, at least not "real" in the sense with which we are familiar.

Everything in the universe in which we live is being manufactured by us. They are ideas rendered into existence; the determination of this rendering relies on our ever-changing direction within the Multi-verse. In other words, your choices determine which aspects of the Multi-verse you render into your existence. Every conceivable possibility is possible, even the most improbable possibilities exist in a universe somewhere within the

Multi-verse. Your subconscious mind merely navigates you through the Multi-verse to fulfill your conscious desires. But to utilize your subconscious mind, you must first be able to communicate with it at a conscious level. To do that, you must first believe that it is possible.

We send messages to our subconscious mind everyday. We do it without even thinking about it. "When it rains it pours", we say to ourselves when things aren't going well. We say or think a statement like that to ourselves and the negativity is the message that gets through to our subconscious mind. What does it do? It directs us towards areas within the Multi-verse where more problems exist for us. Eventually, the problems are solved or become less important to us. It is only when we forget about them because we are preoccupied with something else or place less importance on the negativity that things change for the better. When we become focused on the positive, we often say or think to ourselves, "Okay, things are getting better" or even send a positive message to our subconscious mind with something as simple as a sigh of relief. That message also gets through, this time re-directing our route to a universe within the Multi-verse where there are fewer problems and less stress.

When we are sick, we tend to dwell on being sick. We tend to announce, "I am so sick", or "I don't feel good" or "I'm getting sick." That message gets through to our subconscious mind as well. We have a negative thought about our condition and off we go to a universe where we are sick. Instead of thinking about being sick, think about being healthy and full of life. If there is someone around you who is sick, try not to touch them, but as reinforcement say to yourself, "I never get sick, I have a wonderful immune system that protects me against germs, and I feel great all of the time." There is no need to knock on wood! Saying this isn't a jinx; this is what your supposed to say! Why have we been taught that positive suggestion is superstitious? Positive suggestion works, think about being healthy and zing!!! Off you go to a universe where you are experiencing perfect health.

There is a lot of debate over holistic medicine in that basically it is no more effective than a placebo. But for the people who understand the power of belief, the placebo's work. Why would anybody want to screw that up? For the people who know without a shadow of a doubt that eating chicken soup cures a cold, the chicken soup will work every time. Not because chicken soup contains a miraculous virus anti-body, but because the person eating the soup believes that it works. They visualize the soup making them feel better and they send that message to their subconscious mind and their subconscious mind takes them to an area within the Multi-verse where they are not sick. All drugs are ultimately placebos. All stimuli that come seemingly from the outside world are nothing more than placebos because (finish it for me) none of this is real. We are projecting the reality around us. We are projecting all remedies from our own minds.

Nobody is ever sick because nobody ever feels anything at all. All of this is a product of your mind. Everything, including your aches and pains are just your imagination. I know for the people who are reading this that are suffering, you probably want to throw this book out of the window and punch me in the face. But I am telling you, that all of your suffering is nothing but a dream. The sickness and the pain you are experiencing is in your mind and once you can embrace this concept you will go to an area within the Multi-verse where the pain is gone. I am not trivializing your suffering. Getting to this place of acceptance so that you can cure yourself is the most difficult thing you will ever do in your life. If you are hurting, the pain you are experiencing is a constant reminder of your experience. It is extremely difficult to just accept the fact that it isn't real because it feels real all of the time. But just as the world you see before your eyes is not real, neither is the pain.

About ten years ago someone turned me on to Echinacea Root, an herbal remedy that supposedly builds up the human immune system. I was told that as soon as you feel the slightest sickness coming on or feel that you were exposed to someone who was sick and feared that you might have caught the virus, that you should take a bunch of this stuff and it will help your body resist the oncoming illness. I bought into this idea and to my amazement this stuff worked! I didn't get sick for 2 years. I didn't catch anything, not a single cold or even a sniffle. Whenever I felt illness coming on I took the herbal remedy and the next morning I felt great.

Then one day I was watching the negative infested television news, something that I now make a point to never watch, and up comes a story about the placebo effects of Echinacea Root. From then on, every time my doubt infested mind tried to make use of the root the remedy stopped working for me. I have since convinced myself over the last couple of years that whether it is a placebo or not, the root does work and I concentrate on it working.

Becoming God

I visualize it working for me and I visualize myself healthy the following morning. Echinacea Root does wonders for me now, but it still does not work as well as it once did. I need a new placebo. I need someone to convince me that homemade chocolate chip cookies are the ultimate remedy for any illness.

We communicate with our subconscious mind every minute of everyday whether we are consciously aware of it or not. The problem is most of the time we are not consciously aware of it. This kind of communication is the equivalent of driving a car with a blindfold on. We unconsciously react to our reality and that reaction is the only information our subconscious mind (our navigator through the Multi-verse) has to decide how to get us to our desired universe. To demonstrate this I would like for you now to dredge up some uncomfortable memories. I want you now to think back to a period in your life where things went really bad for you. You can most certainly recall at the time one or two things going wrong and then progressively things got worse in a snowball of unlucky events. Your life became out of your control. You experienced one unfortunate thing after another, until finally it was too much for you and you stopped caring, you stopped dwelling on it. As soon as you stopped focusing on the negativity in your life, and stopped sending negative messages to your subconscious mind, only then did things begin to turn around for you.

For example, allow me to paint a scenario to describe how we currently communicate with our subconscious mind and how it complies with our requests whether we want it to or not. This fictitious scenario would probably drive anyone of us into a sea of hopelessness and permanent doubt.

Welcome To You

One morning you wake up only to discover that your alarm clock did not go off as planned and now you are running very late. In a panic, you jump out of bed and stub your toe on your bedroom furniture, at which you think or say out loud an expletive (!@%$!). This message gets sent to your subconscious mind where it complies with your request sending you directly to another universe where more negative things are happening to you. You start getting dressed, you can't find matching socks or your panty hose get a nasty run in them. Your keys are no longer where you thought you left them, and you can't help at this point to send further requests to go to a universe where shit is really going bad for you. You merge onto the expressway only to discover it to be a parking lot. There are cars beeping, drivers screaming, and middle fingers flying. The morning radio shock Jock is bitching about politics again, which just intensifies the negative messages all around you. Just when you think you can't take anymore of it, you look into your rear-view mirror to the dismay of a policeman pulling you over for an expired tag. You arrive at work but your briefcase is still at home, your boss gives you a lecture, you're not getting the promotion you were counting on, etc., etc. When you reach your breaking point, one of two things happen: You either laugh at the thought of how awful your day has been which sends a message to your subconscious mind to take you back to a universe where you have happiness and control over your life or, you acknowledge your demise sending further requests to your subconscious who complies by brining you to the abyss of stress, failure, and disappointment until you ultimately slip into a nervous breakdown.

For those who don't know, when you have a nervous breakdown you become so emotionally overwhelmed with your problems you cannot dedicate anymore conscious thought to them. You simply give up. When this breakdown takes place, you surrender everything that you are. You let go of your control, which encompasses your identity, your ego, and your conscious self. After you do this, it's almost as if the observer has hit the reset button on your life and the problems vanish before your eyes. The problems still exist, but their significance is no longer important; after all, what could be worse to you then death? If you are lucky, you follow the path your subconscious mind is whispering to you and you leave behind a universe that nearly got the best of you. I challenge that this "reset" condition is not a nervous breakdown, but instead a nervous breakthrough. Unfortunately, for some, their ego does not embrace this newfound enlightenment. For many, it is not long before they once again gain back their confidence and with it their identity. They let go of the power they have been given by handing more and more control back to their conscious self, and once again get sucked back into the never ending dramas of a false reality.

Positive suggestion and surrendering your conscious ego are the *keys* to a successful and blissful life experience. What I mean by a "conscious ego" is the ego that you have accepted through the course of your life. This is a conditional self-identity. More than likely, this self-identity who you have come to know as "you", is not who you really are. Instead your ego is the identity imprinted upon you by societies expectations, cultural tolerance, your parents, friends, spouse, etc. In order to better communicate with your subconscious mind you have to be able to first recognize it as the only link to your true self-identity. Your subconscious mind is always in touch with your true self. It knows your thoughts, your passions, and your purpose in life. You must find your true self and embrace and accept that person for who you really are before you will be truly open to the suggestions being whispered to you by your subconscious mind. Your subconscious mind is under constant guidance from your true identity.

Embracing your conscious ego, on the other hand, closes the door to your subconscious mind and stifles the inspiration and guidance that you are receiving from our collective source. Despite this, many psychotherapists treat their patients by instructing them to do just this. Psychotherapists often encourage embracing the person who you *think* you are regardless of what others may think. The common suggestion being: *"You must love yourself before others will love you"*. By understanding what makes your ego tick, therapists believe that the root source of many psychological problems can be discovered. They believe that finding ways to resolve these pent up issues or memories is the truest road to curing a patient. This is a noble concept and it helps a lot of people. I truly believe psychotherapists want to help their patients, but I believe the method that they are using to achieve this is ultimately wrong. Instead, we must consider therapy through the scope of the Multi-verse theory, which encompasses the idea of a collective identity at the core of ones self. By accepting the realization that you are connected to everything in your reality and furthermore have control over it because you are creating it, you remove the conscious interference between your subconscious mind and your desires. Carl Jung, who I discussed earlier in this book, was convinced that by connecting ourselves to the world around us we would obtain balance, peace and harmony. Jung argued that the ego is an illusion, that at the core we are all connected to a single source. By understanding that everything in your life (good or bad) is being created by you allows for you to ask different questions about why you have chosen, consciously or not, to bring these things or people into your life. By asking these questions, we begin to peel away at our ego and discover what our true purpose in life is meant to be.

It is your conscious identity that grounds you to the reality around you. Identifying yourself, as someone separate from the reality around you is the glue that perpetuates the illusion that reality is something that is happening to you. The reality of it is, you are the reality happening to your ego. To put it even more simply, you are everything around you happening to your body and conscious self. There is no separate self in your universe. You are the thoughts generating the reality around you. You have created a self, a conscious mind to connect those experiences together. There is a saying, *"The world is what we make it"*. I cannot think of a better or more profound idea to accurately represent the true nature of our lives. Good or bad, we make our own reality.

Letting go of you conscious self is a liberating experience but it can also be a very scary idea for most of us. To think that up until this moment the course of your life might be a mistake is a hard pill to swallow. But in the end, knowing that you are serving your intended purpose is what really matters and discovering this is never too late. Most of us don't know who we really are.

Sometimes it takes something as monumental as a "nervous breakthrough" to put things into perspective. It did for me. I went down a very dark road for a while and in the midst of my nervous breakthrough I realized for the first time in my life what really mattered. The first thing that I learned is that I mattered. I learned that my intentions should be what I desire them to be, not the desires that meet other peoples expectations. I learned that I am not my job or how much money I make, or how many accolades I have on the wall. I learned that I am not my family. I learned that who I am is what makes me happy and what inspires me most. It is the things that I live for that define me. I learned too that I serve a purpose, a purpose to serve the ever-growing mind of the universe itself. To put it more majestically, I learned that God had a purpose in mind for me. I learned that by embracing my purpose I got closer to God and closer to my true self. By embracing my purpose and true self-identity, I am closer to happiness than I have ever been and I truly understand for the first time the experience of love and appreciation for living.

You don't need to have a nervous breakthrough though to get in touch with your true self. There are many ways to discover who you are and what your purpose is. For me, unplugging all together from the daily routines of life was the defining moment in my life. The day after my nervous breakthrough I took a Sabbatical. A Sabbatical is a journey, but it is very different from a vacation. Derived from the word Sabbath, a Sabbatical is more of a journey inward than a journey outward. When we take a vacation, we usually share it with family or friends. Our vacations are usually strategically planned and filled with activities. We

Becoming God

would not want to "waste" a single moment of our precious vacation time. Some people do plan a relaxing vacation, which is the right idea, but few of us know how to truly unplug ourselves from our responsibility and our instinctive protection of our conscious ego. Instead a Sabbatical does just that. A Sabbatical is a solo journey. Going solo means limited conversation allowing for more focus and contemplation of the self. Sabbaticals do not have to be elaborate vacations to isolated regions. You can take a sabbatical in your mind simply by going for a walk in a park, or even sitting in an empty room. The key is being alone and unplugging your self from the drama that besieges us every day of our lives.

During your Sabbatical it is important to not concern yourself with anything other than your focus, which is discovering who you are and what your intention is in this life regardless of where that journey might lead you. It is in this quiet time that you contemplate your thoughts, listen to your inner-self, and follow your intuition. Open your mind to whatever suggestion is being whispered into your ear. Take special consideration to the ideas that occur to you the most and then act on them, no matter how ridiculous the idea might be. Despite how this may sound, these thoughts and ultimate actions are not reckless or selfish. At the end of every consideration this is ultimately your life and no one else's. Satisfying our personal needs is how we become self-aware which is the key to consciously or lucidly creating our own reality.

You might ask if we are creating our reality, why then would we create problems for ourselves? Why would we render stress in our lives? Why would we render illness, or pain, or unfortunate events? Why would we render anything but a fairy-tale of a life? I would suggest to you that there are two reasons. One, is that we simply don't know any better; we have never been shown an alternate way of living and we are simply addicted to or find comfort in familiarity. Two, is that we are programmed to do so. Perhaps we are directed or guided by some source deep with in our superconscious to render certain types of lives over and over again in order to learn from them, or even more logically, to see if we can break free from them. We would create this challenge simply to make a game out of it because routinely manifesting a perfect life would eventually get boring. More than anything there is no way to truly appreciate divinity without sometimes encountering struggle and challenge.

Addiction to an aspect of our reality is exactly the same as an addiction to anything else. The mechanism that makes us addicted to drugs is the same mechanism that makes us addicted to our emotions. Drugs are in affect, physiologically rendering amplified stimulations of a particular emotion. Ecstasy renders a stimulation of the emotions connected with love, empathy and a child like innocence. Cocaine renders a stimulation of confidence; Heroine renders the stimulation of apathy, shutting down the emotions entirely, as with marijuana to a lesser degree. What we are addicted to is not the drug. We are addicted to the emotion that the drug stimulates. The mechanism for how we stimulate all of our emotions is physiologically the same.

Some people are addicted to or find comfort in sadness and depression. Some are addicted to feeling inferior or having a lack of self-confidence. Some people are addicted to the feeling of being abused. It is not uncommon at all for a battered wife to seek out another abusive situation after breaking free of the previous one. Some people are addicted to power and having power over others. Some are addicted to being abusive to others. This is why our lives seem to be re-plays of the same experiences and problems over and over again. It is the reason why we keep finding ourselves in the same relationships, around the same types of people and friends, and in the same types of jobs. Our experiences repeat themselves over and over because whether the experiences are positive or negative, they are familiar and comfortable to us. These experiences evoke the emotions that we are addicted to.

It is our comfort and addiction to emotions that keeps us from rendering an alternate reality for ourselves. We recreate the same experiences until we consciously make a determined choice to break free of those experiences by sending that message to our subconscious selves. Breaking free from our emotional addictions is difficult. Breaking free requires us to eliminate the single emotion that controls us and keeps us bound to our addictions and familiar experiences. That emotion is *fear*. More than anything we fear the uncertain, we fear change and we fear failure. But with the realization that we are the sum of our experiences, fear needs to be embraced because fear is just a part of you. You cannot fail because there is nothing to fail. There is no uncertainty because you are manifesting your reality. Fear is merely: <u>F</u>alse <u>E</u>vidence <u>A</u>ppearing <u>R</u>eal.

It is my belief that by rendering an alternate reality for our selves through belief in the mechanics of the multi-verse and through meditation, we can overcome our illusion of fear and become addicted to positive things like love, praise, success or whatever makes you happy. You deserve to live the happiest, most exciting, exhilarating life imaginable, all you have to do is believe that you deserve it and the change will happen.

Manifesting change in your life requires both determination and discomfort, but more than anything it requires trust. Like with any addiction, breaking away from experiences that evoke emotions that satisfy our urges is difficult. Your body will physically go through the same withdraw you would experience in giving up any other kind of addiction. But more than this (and this is the difficult part) you need to let go of you.

Remind yourself that "you" are your experiences. You must let go of your inhibitions and take chances. Ask yourself what you really want out of life. Ask yourself what do you really have to loose if all of this is just a dream? Your life doesn't have to be extraordinary to have meaning, but at the very least you need to become aware of what the meaning of your life is. To do this is to understand your life's purpose. Why cherish a meaningless life? An uninspired life is a waste of your experience within the Multi-verse. Make your life count! You should try thinking about your life as a video game. The worst thing that can happen to you in the world is that you fail to obtain your desired goal or worse your body dies, both are just experiences within a false reality.

I don't believe that the death of our body is such a big deal at all. I believe that death is merely a transition from one dimension to the next in an infinite cycle. It isn't that I don't have appreciation for life, because I have tremendous appreciation for it.

Becoming God

I would not have an interest in this subject and I certainly would not be writing this book if I didn't have enormous appreciation for life. But for me, I truly believe that this is all just a game. For me, this is all just a test and the challenge is to make the fullest life possible before you can move on to the next higher plane of existence. This is my variation on the Buddhist ideology. There is a famous bumper sticker that says *"Ye who dies with the most toys wins."* How about instead: *"Ye who dies with the most experiences or most exhilarating life wins."*

Your life is not about "you". Take your ego out of the equation. You are an observer and the observer resides somewhere outside of your body. Your life, your reality is not about the person you see in the mirror. The part that is you, your being, are the thoughts that make up your experiences. You are the reality around you. You are not your body. Your body is like a glove, a sock puppet. It is merely the virtual interface or instrument that you, your subconscious self (true self), utilizes to interact with and to contemplate your thoughts and ideas. The world you see around you is merely an elaborate set built by you for your puppet to act out your own fantasies in. The truth is, you got so caught up being in the role of the sock puppet that you forgot that you were play-acting. How funny is that?

This is a radical philosophy and these are very scary thoughts to some of you. Many of you will think that what I am saying is reckless. Perhaps it is. Maybe I am wrong. Maybe we get one shot at life and we need to make the best of it. If this is the case and we do indeed only get one shot at life, then I am going for it! I am letting everything go and I am going for the best experience possible and if I fail or die in the process then that will be my experience. I have no use for a mundane existence. For me, if I only have the money to play one game, I am picking the most exciting game that I can find. On the other hand, I can understand someone who would seek out the easiest game that would provide the longest playtime. The choice, like everything in your reality is yours. But remember, time itself is an illusion.

Imagine a world or a society who instead of religious beliefs being instilled into their psyche from the very beginning, they where taught this very basic ideology. These people are taught about the Multi-verse and the mechanics of it. Instead of the Bible, they are taught about the power of their subconscious mind and its ability to direct them to different areas within the Multi-verse and thus to a different life. These people are taught that anything they desire is possible and can be achieved by sheer will alone. This society has never come in contact with anyone outside of his or her culture or with any contradictory beliefs. Their power over their subconscious mind would be limitless because they would believe in themselves unconditionally having never encountered anything that would instill a seed of doubt. The people here understand very clearly how to achieve the maximum life experience. These people are game masters. It sounds like a wonderful place and many of us wish that we could live there, and we do! This is not a fantasy world. There is no doubt that a world like this, many worlds like this, exist within the Multi-verse, even worlds like this where you exist within in them and where you too are a game master. We can create a world like this right here, right now.

Becoming God

Many of our current thoughts about life are assumptions we have made do to our conditioning. We do things or think about things without even knowing why we do it. Our imagination has been stifled with the illusion of fear and social expectations. Instead of individuality being freely expressed, most of us are so desperate to conform to our surroundings and to the expectations of others we forget who we really are. The real irony is asking yourself; if you are creating your own reality just whom are you conforming for? On the contrary, children come into this world full of imagination, awe, and playful disregard. They are the closest things to our true source. We teach them to conform because we want the best for them, but limiting the imagination is not the road to happiness. In schools, less and less importance is placed on encouraging individuality. We make children wear uniforms for conformity, we limit lessons in artistic, music, and theatrical forms of expression, and we are obsessed with testing children's comprehension of rules in mathematics and grammar. Instead, our focus should be on encouraging self-expression and original thought. We should make a game out of everything, allowing moderate rule bending to encourage thinking outside of the box. I believe that we could learn more from the children then they could ever learn from us. Instead of teaching children "No", (which stifles creativity and imagination) teach them, "Know" (encouraging them to figure out alternate ways to get what they desire). In explaining to any child the reasons why they need to know what the obstacle is, you will often recognize that there really isn't an obstacle at all, we have just been conditioned to believe that there is. It is in small changes like these that we could change the world. Until now we have been treating the symptom to the problem with our expectation of others, enforcing rules and establishing laws. Instead we need to treat the cause, encouraging individuality and focusing on ourselves. People will always do what's right for them and because we are one, that will ultimately be what's right for us all.

The seemingly insignificance of our lives in this universe, can be an extremely uncomfortable thought. To think that with all that we are our life is just some virtual reality or that we are just someone else's dream is heartbreaking. But a different perception changes everything. The proverbial glass of water is either half empty or half full. I asked you earlier in this book to question for yourselves what it is to really live, or to really exist? As Descartes showed us, your experience *is* existing. You are alive and your collective experiences are the meaning of your life. How magnificent a life to be able to manifest your own reality! This is far more exciting than a "real" life, living in an organic world of solid matter. We create our own lives. *We are God!*

There is no one to look to for praise or punishment we are that majesty. There is no right or wrong. There is no Karma. It is not possible for you to hurt other people because there are no other people! The other people are all you. By hurting them you are only hurting yourself. This is all your reality. This is all your creation. I am not saying its okay to start breaking laws and commandments, and start hurting and killing one another, because those behaviors are simply counter productive. You wouldn't allow one hand to hurt or steal from your other hand, rightly so by hurting other people you are only hurting yourself. It is your ego creating the illusion that you are separate from others, when in fact we are the same being. Instead, you should want to choose experiences that evolve you as an entity. You should want to manifest a reality that elevates you and allows you to grow as a being. Your purpose in life should be to become self-aware, to awaken to the realization that you are God.

Growth is the single greatest way that we can serve God who *is* our Universal Mind. We should make it our purpose in life to constantly grow by keeping an open mind, changing our opinions, learning new things, exploring new ways to stimulate our bodies, seeing new places, making new friends, changing aspects of our personality, etc. Growing is part of the life process. We are designed to grow, because that too serves our purpose.

Successful people come in all shapes and sizes. They can be ugly, they can be beautiful, they can be rich or they can be poor. They can be nice and selfless or they can be selfish and mean, even down right evil. Often times "bad" people or just plain assholes are successful. They are successful because they are playing the game regardless of consequence. They are good to themselves and they feel positive about their actions. Some people are successful at everything they do. Even they don't know how, but luck just seems to follow them everywhere. It is my suspicion that they are beginning to master the Multi-verse and with it their life experience. Perhaps they are "old souls" or they simply have played this game a million times or more and each time they learn just a little bit more about how to successfully manifest their reality even if they are not consciously aware of it.

I have been privileged to meet many successful people through the course of my life. The most interesting part about each of them is even if they weren't successful at what brought them this success they would be doing the same occupation anyway. Each found inspiration in something and miraculously luck just seemed to find each of them. These aren't coincidences. These people chose to follow their heart even at times when the people around them were directing them somewhere different. It was preposterous for me to think that I had any chance at all of making it in the music business. I had limited talent, no connections, and little, if any, outside support. But being successful wasn't a concern for me. I knew that I was supposed to make music with my life. I knew with more certainty than anything else in my life that I was supposed to focus on music and nothing else. It was the only thing that "felt" right. I'm not going to say that I didn't dream of success, but finding success was not my preoccupation. My passion was for expressing my emotions through music. My passion was for communicating those feelings to others through my music. I believed in what I was doing. I believed that I was making the right choices, and I knew that everything would take care of it self and it did.

At the end of your life however, material things do not measure success. Materialism is useless because you can't take any of it with you. Instead of concentrating on guiding yourself to an area within the Multi-verse where you have won the lottery, think about the ways that you can manipulate the reality around you in lasting meaningful ways. Manifest a reality that will provoke completely original ideas and original experiences. Mastering your

Becoming God

ability to change reality by sheer will alone is the ultimate goal. We should all strive to become a Messiah, a master of the universe. What is the fun in playing God if you're not going to utilize your abilities?

Accepting this new philosophy often surfaces new fears. The first fear (illusion) is that; if people didn't have Karma or Sin to worry about, everyone would just go around robbing and hurting others to get what they want the simplest way. By accepting this philosophy you must know by now that no one can hurt you except for you. When you are the master of your reality nobody else can have any affect on you at all unless you want them to. In addition to this, the world we live in is a fairytale and it is infinitely abundant. It is way more fun to manifest a perfect reality for yourself than to steal it from someone else. There is no better feeling in the world than accomplishment over your reality. The second fear (illusion) is that if everyone followed their dreams, there would be no one left to be responsible and keep the world running. The word responsible means "able to respond". Ask yourself; are you responding (reacting) to your experience or are you in control over it by creating it? I'm in control of every aspect of my reality and I am thus insulated from anything that can harm me. The world will continue to revolve around me should I ask it to and it will do the same for you. *"Truly, truly I say to you, he who believes in me will also do the works that I do; and greater works than these will he do."*

See the figure on page 220 for further understanding.

"When you recognize that there is a voice in your head that pretends to be you and never stops speaking, you are awakening out of your unconscious identification with the stream of thinking. When you notice that voice, you realize that who you are is not the voice - the thinker - but the one who is aware of it. Knowing yourself as the awareness behind the voice is freedom."

~Eckhart Tolle

Chapter 9:

Manifesting Your Reality

Practical Exercises To Show You
That You Master Your Own Reality

Becoming God

I'm going to give you a little test for you to perform to show you in a very immediate way the communication process between your conscious and your subconscious mind. As I have said many times, belief is the key to achieving success in communicating with your subconscious mind. Obviously, the less significant or remarkable the request, the less stretch of the imagination it is for you to believe. Belief for anyone should first come with supportive evidence and it should be reinforced by experimentation. Here is a simple experiment for you to try on your own that will help you build credibility for the powers that I have suggested are within your grasps.

Before going to bed as you lie there under the covers in the dark, I want you to think repeatedly about a clock. See the clock in your minds eye and visualize the current time. It is important that you visualize a clock that you are familiar with, for example, the clock on your night-stand or bedroom wall; a clock that you see all of the time or a clock that you are likely to see when you first wake up. I find it easier to think about an analog clock, the kind with hands, but most are familiar with the digital kind.

Now, I want you to concentrate very hard on the visualization of the clock displaying the current time. Think about that picture for a moment and say the time to yourself or out loud preferably. Now think about a time in the morning that you want to get up. To reinforce the power of the suggestion, it would be better for you to think about an unusual time for you to wake up. Pick something crazy like 4:30 am or something. Now imagine, very slowly, your imagined clock moving forward in time briefly pausing at a quarter after each our, then at half past each hour, then at a quarter 'til and so on until you have reached your desired wake up time. As the clock moves, think to yourself about the time and say out loud or in your head each of the pause times as they pass. Keep a calm tone in your voice or inner voice. When you reach your desired wake up time, concentrate on the visualization of the clock displaying that time. Say to yourself repeatedly, I am awake at 4:30 am or whatever your chosen time is. Continue to concentrate. Imagine yourself wide-awake; more awake then you have ever been at your desired time. Repeat the process until you fall asleep. When your desired time arrives, you will be wide-awake.

So how did this work? It works because you got through to your subconscious mind. You established a communication link with your subconscious and gave it instructions to take you to a universe where you would wake up at 4:30 am. Near by this universe there is a universe where you wake up at 4:31 am. A little further away is a universe where you wake up at 4:15 am. Much, much further away lie universes where you wake up in a completely different bed and time altogether.

If this were true, one might ask, why we can't just imagine ourselves going to a universe with such significant differences such as waking up in a different bed with a different life. The answer is we can. Anything is possible. There are occasions in our lives where we may visualize a significant change such as waking up in a different bed with a different life and our subconscious mind is directed towards that goal, towards that universe, and begins the steps to progressively get us there. It is also possible to jump to the

Becoming God

universes directly because any possibility is possible within the Multi-verse, however, having the belief that we can actually convince our subconscious mind to take us to this place overnight requires a bigger stretch of the imagination, a much greater suspension of disbelief. More than likely doubt would prevail in your conscious mind and as a result you would fail to communicate your desire to your subconscious mind.

Controlling your direction within the Multi-verse gets easier with practice. The best retention for learning anything is through learning things in baby steps. So, for the next baby step, we're going to manifest quarters. I think it's safe to assume that most of us would like to have a little more money. I'm sure some would like to have a whole lot more, but manifesting large sums of money requires a bigger suspension of disbelief. To practice manifesting money, first try to manifest finding abandoned quarters. Think about it, how often do you really find a quarter? You may find pennies, nickels and dimes maybe, but a quarter? - Almost never. Try this for a month until you have nearly a jar full of quarters, and then up the ante to finding dollars, then five dollars and so on. I am currently up to $40.

For another test, study the affects of your attitude and in particular, your words on another person. You can best observe your affects with someone who doesn't appear to be having a good day. I do this all of the time and I find the joy that it brings me to change someone's attitude for the better is amazing to say the least. Last week for example, I approached a woman behind the deli counter just before closing. As a former deli worker myself, when I was in my teens, I remembered how irritating it was to have a customer come in at near closing and order an elaborate sandwich. As I approached the counter, Betty rolled her eyes so that I could see that she was irritated. She stopped what she was doing abruptly and in the most condescending tone, she asks, "Can I help you?" Instead of being offended by her attitude toward a paying customer, I chose to smile at her and I greeted her by name with the most positive attitude I could muster. I gave her my order making a light joke where I could. While she was making my sandwich, I told her I remember the days of working behind the counter and how awful it was when a customer came in as we were closing. I briefly told her how I had a long day and that I knew one of her special sandwiches would brighten my day. Betty was now making my sandwich with the greatest care. I continued to carry on a conversation forcing any issue I could think of. By the time she was slicing my sandwich in half she had a smile from ear to ear and she was now engaging in the conversation. I learned that she was excited to see her son who was coming home from college over the weekend and that they were planning a nice trip to the mountains for an old fashioned family outing. After handing me my sandwich Betty asked with a smile, "What is your name?" I told her that my name was Ford and she told me what a pleasure it was to meet me. She added with a smile, that I had made her day.

      Kindness is infectious. Dispensing it will only bring it back to you. Go out of your way to be kind to one another and you will often find a bumpy start. But remember, the rougher the start, the greater the pay off. It feels amazing to turn these kinds of situations around. The slightest effort that I dispensed on my part with Betty in the beginning was rewarded to me ten fold with a smile and a delightful conversation that made me feel incredible. It is hard sometimes to put on a smile when we are inundated with negative situations and negative people. In these situations, I make a game out of it. I make a game of finding ways to put myself into a better mood and I make a game out of turning someone's attitude around. I do this more so to help me feel better. Helping them feel better is merely the bonus aspect of the game. By keeping a positive attitude within and even more so exuding a positive attitude, I am concretely sending messages to my subconscious mind telling it exactly what I want out of life. I am taking over the wheel driving myself directly towards the universes filled with positive people in my life and a universe that holds a positive attitude within myself. I rarely loose my game, but in the cases where I do loose I just pick another person. Unfortunately, the world has become infected with negativity and impersonal interaction. It doesn't take long to find a target for the next game.

We know that our subconscious mind is open to suggestion. This is the reason hypnosis works. It is also the reason that much of psychotherapy works. The experiments I gave you to perform work because you are sending a message to your subconscious mind. Master the communication process between your conscious mind and your subconscious mind and you will become a master of the universe. There are no limitations to the possibilities you can achieve once that communication process has been firmly established.

Your subconscious mind is waiting and is open to suggestion whether those suggestions are negative or positive. As I have said before, your subconscious mind does not differentiate between good or bad, negative or positive. Your subconscious mind only knows experience. All experiences to your subconscious mind are growth, for its mission is only in gathering information through those experiences and learning something about itself from your interaction with it. When your reaction to experience causes you to ask your subconscious to manifest a different experience, it will most certainly comply. Having a clearer understanding of the true nature of your reality and with it the ability to manifest alternate realities will only make the learning more interesting. You might then ask, if this is possible why don't we see other people flying around like superman and moving things around with their minds? If it is possible to successfully master this communication process and hence master the universe, why don't we see others doing this? The answer I'm afraid, you are not going to like. One possible answer is because the other people do not exist. You manifest all the other people in your reality.

This idea of ultimate solitude is extremely uncomfortable for most people, so much so that many have embraced an alternate theory. Right now there are two opposing camps of thought when considering the nature of our reality. One camp believes that every conscious being is collectively co-creating and sharing the reality around us. For example, my wife and I share the same reality along with everyone else we encounter. If we were to go to a park in the afternoon one day, she might be manifesting some trees and green grass and I might be manifesting things that I associate with a park, such as a large playground and ducks in a pond. The other people in the background are also co-creating different aspects of our shared reality in the park. In this sense, reality is not much different from the way in which we currently experience it other than the reality we collectively see is fluid and completely dependent on how we choose to manifest it collectively. In this scenario it is possible that the reason we don't see miraculous feats being achieved solely due to positive imaging is because either we don't believe it is possible as a collective group or perhaps because we collectively co-create our reality under the guidelines of certain rules, such as we can create anything we wish within our shared dream state as long as it does not defy our particular laws of physics for this particular dream. However, to me this idea places too much humanistic quality on something that is in all probability humanly incomprehensible. Rules? Since when do dreams have rules? I can recount many dreams were I have defied the laws of physics by flying around like superman, travel spontaneously to various locations instantly, had multiple perspectives of the same dream and further incredible feats. Why should our waking dream be any different?

The other camp of thought on the contrary, believes that our waking reality is no different from the dreams when we sleep. The thought is we are experiencing a dream during our "waking hours" and we are creating all aspects of our reality including the other people using our own imagination just as we do in our dreams when we sleep. The other people exist; they just don't exist in your dream state. Each of us is the master of our own separate dream state, and we are connected through our source. When we encounter other people, we are each experiencing the connection through our source. An analogy would be similar to a videoconference. We can see and speak to each other, but the interaction is transmitted through our source. This is possible because our source is exactly that, it is our source. The super-conscious is the source of all egos because we are a single conscious being dreaming of becoming separate individuals. Many argue that we simply could not be this creative, but this argument hardly holds up when considering how vastly imaginative our dreams are when we sleep. We invent other people all of the time and we create wildly original settings and experiences. For many this concept is less appealing simply because it suggests that we are alone. It is a terrifying thought to think that we are completely alone in this world, even if we are creating it. With that being said, this theory, as uncomfortable as it may seem, explains why we do not encounter other people fully manifesting ideal realities. We do not encounter them because we do not believe (in this particular dream state) that it's possible and thus don't create other people doing this. Another argument to this theory is that our "waking reality" seems more "real" than our dreams. I would argue that it only seems more real because this is the dream we are in now. When you experience any dream at all, the experience of the dream while you are experiencing it is entirely real to you no matter how bizarre they may seem. It only seems unreal to us when the dream is over. When the dream of our waking life ceases, we will most likely remember this life as just another dream.

Ultimately, reality is random information and thoughts forming dreams within dreams within another dream continuing for infinity. The dream in which you currently reside is equally as profound as it is insignificant and meaningless. What I mean is, in the context of this current dream everything has meaning. Every

Becoming God

single aspect of your reality is symbolic or is a metaphor to remind you that you are dreaming. Outside of the waking dream however, everything you just experienced within this dream is completely meaningless adding only to the compilation of experience to our ever-growing conscious mind. This is how the universe comprehends anything and everything. Our current dream provides profound experiences and knowledge to our collective source and yet is merely a gesture in a complex ballet of infinite dreams providing new understanding and new perspective. In the barren of infinity, dreaming is something for God to do; it is a method of expression. It is through dreaming that God can appreciate his own magnificence.

In this concept, you are everything around you. Your being or soul *is* your experience. Everything in your reality is a projection from inside of your mind and not necessarily a mind that is geographically located between your ears - you have no ears! Remember, the person you see in the mirror does not exist either. "You" are merely a collection of thoughts and everything in your reality is your creation. Even this book that you are holding in your hand and that you are reading is a projection from you. The ideas proposed in this book that are blowing your mind away are your own ideas. Perhaps the information in this book is information already gathered by your subconscious mind in an effort to guide you to new areas within the Multi-verse so that you may gain new experiences. Perhaps this book is your symbolic metaphor, your calling card to get off of the couch, turn off the T.V. and make something incredible of your life. If you could dream for anything why would you dream to be anything less than a master of your universe?

Can we manifest anything we want by sheer will alone? Of course we can! However, more than just *believing* that you can, you have to *know* that you can; and knowing requires far more trust in yourself than just believing. All of our beliefs are based on the most plausible solution to satisfy our "gut instinct" which is different for everyone. You can believe in something that satisfies 95% of your gut instinct. However, 95% is not knowing, there is still 5% left over for doubt. The only way to truly know anything at all is through experience. To gain this experience, you must follow your heart and intuition wherever it leads you regardless of what anyone or anything is telling you otherwise. Each time you pursue your own intuition with confidence and invigoration, you are testing the theory; and with each successful test you will gain more confidence in your beliefs. It is within this confidence and harmony with your true self, that you will *know* everything.

You need to have *faith* in your new understanding to believe it, and you must test it to know it. Yes, it is stupendously ironic that you must first abandon all of your faith just to gain it back. But the irony is just an illusion because this time your faith didn't come packaged in doubt.

"We are not human beings who have occasional spiritual experiences – it's the other way around: we're spiritual beings that have occasional human experiences."

~Deepak Chopra

Chapter 10:
Manifesting Techniques

Meditation, Visualization,
The Law of Attraction and Lucid Dreaming

Becoming God

There are a lot of different ideas and methods for communicating with your subconscious mind and tapping into the Multi-verse. How effective the methods are is indeed the question, but the effectiveness of any of these methods relies on the same single requirement and that requirement is belief.

The Buddhist and Hindu believe that meditation is the best method for communing with God. The Christians, Muslims, Jews and many other religions believe that prayer is the answer. As strange as meditation may sound to some of you, it really isn't all that different from prayer. Prayer can be thought of as just another form of meditation. In both methods we close our eyes and concentrate on our message for God. The Buddha insist that meditation alone is not enough. They believe that meditation is only effective when you live and practice the Buddhist life style, essentially being good to yourself and good to others. This ideology is not so different from the other religions. For example, any good Christian will tell you that prayer alone is not enough, you must first be a good Christian which goes the same for the Muslims, Jews and other religions who choose prayer as the primary communication with God. My view is that being good is probably the right idea. After all every action you take is ultimately toward yourself. However, I don't believe that being "good" is criteria for manifesting your reality. In the end, gaining experience (good or bad) is all that really matters.

The Freemasons believe in the practice of The Law of

Attraction, which suggests putting your wishes out there into the universe by keeping a state of mind that attracts the things you want out of life. They believe in writing out wish lists, replacing negative thoughts with positive ones, and other various visualization techniques. Though this practice has been around for centuries, only now can we truly appreciate from a scientific perspective the intuitive connection they made between positive thinking and the realization of your dreams. This practice is even easier to apply by keeping a positive attitude, and by staying consciously aware that what we are experiencing is only a product of our imagination. By continually reinforcing and accepting the fact we are living in a dream, which can be manipulated by our will is a step towards eliminating doubt; an elimination of the doubt that is the wall between your conscious mind and your subconscious mind. I find it interesting that Freemason's believe that this is more of a state of mind than simply a practice. This state of mind also included the belief in a worldwide brotherhood that transcends all religious, ethnic, cultural and educational differences.

The Aborigine as well as many psychologists and scientists believe that analyzing, understanding and controlling our dreams through lucid dreaming is the answer to manifesting our desires. It seems to be the consensus that when we dream our conscious mind "goes away" and we are in direct commune with God. It is believed by some that this is the moment when the observer pulls out of the body and out of the Multi-verse. There are also many other people who believe that the only quality time we have for positive suggestion and reinforcement are in those hazy, drifting moments upon first awakening and just before falling asleep. If this is the case, then I would suggest that hypnosis is the answer. Hypnosis is all about putting the body and mind into an ultimate relaxed state similar to the state of body and mind just prior to sleep and post awakening.

Meditation & Visualization

For the Buddhist, Yoga and many New Age believers, meditation is the preferred method of breaking through your barrier of doubt and establishing a communication link between your conscious and subconscious mind.

The traditional Buddhist method of meditation is not as supernatural as it sounds and actually makes a great deal of sense with this new concept of our reality. The idea behind traditional meditation is to concentrate so intensely on a single object that everything else disappears. Because our mind is rendering our reality, by focusing all of our energy and processing power on a single object, the mind no longer attempts to render other aspects of our reality and hence the true nature of reality is revealed to us in our peripheral vision. Remember, quantum mechanics has shown us very clearly that when we are not looking, reality is not there.

Through meditation, it is believed that we peel away the fabric of our reality and expose the true nature of the world that we live in. It is believed that once achieving this heightened state of altered consciousness we become fully aware of ourselves as the observer, accepting this truth and removing our seed of doubt that is interfering with the power of our subconscious. Achieving this level of altered consciousness is said to be extremely difficult, though there are many who claim to have done it with a lot of practice. The most interesting part about the testimonials is that many of the accounts come from Buddhist monks throughout the centuries. Their accounts are exactly what we would expect to find when applied to our view of the new Multi-verse theory.

Probably the most effective method for manifesting our desires is through visualization. In this meditation method visualization becomes the focal point instead of the single object. Visualization is the most effective and practical way to channel the ideas we want to get through to our subconscious. There are hundreds of books about the power of utilizing visualization techniques. There are also hundreds of motivational speakers going around teaching people how to visualize better sales, visualize better health, and visualize a better life for themselves, etc... All of these people have got it right. But where they fail us is in presenting a satisfactory reason as to why the method is so effective. Many just say that you don't need to know why it works, just know that it works. This may be easy for some, but if you are at all like me, I have trouble accepting anything on blind faith alone. My lack of faith is all the doubt that I need to prevent the methods from working for me. It is their lack of a thorough investigation into this process and lack of demonstrating the mechanics of the process, which leaves room in our minds for doubt and as a result breaks the communication process between the conscious and subconscious mind. This is where I hope to offer something different.

This whole book has been leading up to these next few simple ideas and it is imperative that you at least somewhat understand the science and philosophy I have explained up to this point. By understanding the implications of everything that I have discussed in this book the picture should be perfectly clear to you for how and why visualization techniques and positive thinking work. Not only should your new view of the mechanics of reality reinforce your belief in the power of suggestion and visualization it should ask you to reinterpret the method so that you can tweak it to make it work the best for you.

So why and how is visualization so effective? It is effective because when we visualize something, a part of our mind is actually rendering or manifesting that potential reality. As I explained earlier in this book, quantum physics has shown us that every conceivable possibility has the potential for existing. The information for any possible reality is there and waiting for your mind to manifest, or render that potential reality into existence. The visualization of your goal is a potential universe that is now being rendered into existence just by thinking about it. As I have said many times throughout this book, thoughts are things, and your dreams are just as real as your waking reality. By visualizing our goals, we are rendering those potential universes and we are creating that possibility. We are creating an experience and we are instructing our subconscious mind to guide us towards it.

Visualization is essentially day dreaming which ironically,

Manifesting Techniques

is another aspect of our culture that is frowned upon. Visualization sounds fancy and difficult but is something that we all practice everyday of our lives. Anyone can visualize anything. We practice it when we dream, and when we think about anything at all. We practice visualization everyday when we hear a story that someone is telling us. When someone tells us a story, we hear their spoken words and paint a picture to go along with that story in our minds eye. We can visualize a story by reading. We can also visualize something by just imagining it however; it is far more difficult to paint an original picture by just thinking about it. This picture is often fluid, changing every time you think about different aspects of your desire. For this reason, it is important first that you formulate your desire and *release* it from your mind by either writing it down or speaking it out loud. Don't be afraid to share your desires with someone by telling them about it or even recording yourself saying it. When you say it or read it, you are absorbing it for the first time. It is within this absorption that you begin to comprehend it. The processing and contemplation of these desires is the mechanism, which will help you manifest them.

If I were to tell you to think of a purple elephant hanging from a daisy on the edge of a cliff, you would have no trouble at all of closing your eyes and thinking about what I described. Every time we visualize something we are creating. We are partly rendering a possible universe. The picture in our minds eye is no less real than the picture we see in the reality around us when we open our eyes. They are both just as real, which says less for our waking reality than it does more for the existence of purple elephants and super strong daisy's. The visualization however is merely a glimpse into a possible universe. To get there we need to make it more real. We need to think about every detail. But more importantly than anything, in order to get there we need to believe that it is a real place.

I have spoken much of the conscious mind and the subconscious mind throughout this book. I told you that the subconscious mind is your direct connection or link to the reality around you (which is who you are) and that the conscious mind serves as the ego. The purpose of the ego and the conscious mind is to serve as a tool to separate you from your reality. Doing this perpetuates the illusion that reality is something that is happening to you, rather than something you are doing to yourself. It is your conscious mind that is going to block and reject any of your thoughts that you have control over the reality around you. The conscious mind sets up boundaries and enforces rules to keep the experience real to you. That is the job of the conscious mind and it achieves this through self-doubt and fear. The purpose of meditation and visualization is to by-pass the conscious mind and suggest our desires directly to the source of the reality around us, directly to our subconscious mind that is controlling everything in our lives.

You are the way that you see yourself. If you see yourself as bad then you will be bad. If you see yourself as poor then you will be poor. If you see yourself as rich, you will be rich. Your subconscious only knows what you tell it. It is waiting to manifest realities based on your suggestions and visualizations. For example, some people suffer from an inferiority complex. With this understanding of reality you should know that you are not inferior to anyone or anything, but instead you are God. You create the world around you and you are superior to all things in your reality. The people you think you are inferior to are just you. To think of your insecurity as anything else is just an illusion. Your waking life is no more real than the life in your dreams when you sleep.

We have all often heard stories where people do incredible physical feats such as a mother lifting an overturned car to save her children inside it and so on. Achievements such as these are often credited to an increase in the adrenaline production during a moment of stress. But I think more than likely these people are able to do these miraculous things because they visualize themselves doing it. They visualize themselves doing these impossible things without doubt interfering because they have to. They have to perform the impossible and they see only themselves doing it. There is no time for doubt or to visualize failure. They see themselves lifting the car and therefore they do. In reality, the car is no heavier than a feather. It is only our mind that is perpetuating the illusion that the car is heavy. The car does not exist. The car like everything else is only a thought generated by you.

Before anyone broke the 4-minute mile nobody thought that it was humanly possible. Doctors said that it was physically impossible; they claimed that the human heart would explode. People came close, but no one would ever break the barrier. Then one day Roger Banister ran and did the impossible. He ran an entire mile in less than 4 minutes. It was a miracle of physiology. But more important than breaking the 4-minute mile was the fact that Banister proved to the world it was humanly possible. He

Becoming God

raised the bar of doubt. The same year 3 other people broke the 4-minute mile. They accomplished this not out of competition, because the competition was always there. They accomplished this because they not only believed, but they *knew* it was possible. Anything is possible. Every barrier we have ever established in our reality is nothing more than fantasy. If you can dream it and visualize it, you can do it. We are only held back by the limitation of our imagination.

To utilize the visualization method of meditation you need to first figure out what kind of picture you need to manifest in your minds eye that represents the finality of your goal. A picture speaks a thousand words, but finding the picture is not always easy. For me, I found this process to be extremely difficult, probably because I am not a very visual person. I knew what goals I wanted to achieve but found it very difficult to think about them in the sense of a picture or a vision of an obtainable goal.

Let's say for example money is a concern for you and you desire to have more of it. You could simply think of yourself falling into a haystack of cash. But I'm not sure how effective this is going to be because this visualization requires quite a stretch of the imagination (at least for some of us) and doubt would more than likely prevail. Instead, I would take it slowly. I would imagine and visualize your goal or goals in very plausible progressive baby steps. Plausibility is the key here, because before anything you must believe that this is possible.

I would imagine a dream of something good happening to you at work. Maybe you just closed a huge sale, or maybe you gave a great presentation or whatever. The details of the steps to get there are not important, but the details that conjure up the good feelings are. Visualize yourself doing a private celebration and patting yourself on the back. Visualize next getting called into see your boss who is smiling and praising you on a job well done perhaps even giving you a promotion. Focus on the joy and satisfaction that this moment brings you. Visualize holding a check in your hand. The check is more than you would expect to find. You grip the check as if it were a life rope thrown out to you. Visualize yourself depositing the check with the sense of relief that your worries are over. Imagine celebrating with your family or friends. Next visualize that you are buying something nice for yourself, something you have always wanted. Remember the happiness that this brings you. Visualize spreading your newfound happiness with anyone who will receive it.

In each of these visions of your daydream it is important to concentrate on every subtle detail. It is imperative that you make each of your visualizations as real as possible. Include everything from the way things look around you to what you're wearing, the sounds that you hear, the way your surroundings smell, etc. It is the details that make the experience a reality. The more real you make it and the more times you think about it, the closer your subconscious comes to finding it. Don't be afraid to experience your visualizations in your waking life. Try on that dress! Test - drive that new car! Take a stroll through your dream house. Absorb every detail to apply them all towards your visualizations.

Remember, your daydream actually exists somewhere within the Multi-verse. Somewhere there is another you living that moment and by diligently thinking about it you are directing your being towards that moment. You are directing yourself towards those areas of the multi-verse where your dreams play out. As you get closer to your imaged goal you will begin to see your experiences set up the scenario to cause the reality of your day dream to manifest itself into your waking reality. As you get closer and begin to see your dreams become a reality, it is important that you take a step back and note that it was your visualization that made this happen for you. With every successful visualization exercise you will believe more and more in your infinite possibility.

Remember, this is happening because none of it is real. All of it is just a dream. This may sound impossible, but if I were to prescribe this method to you as way to alter your dreams while you were a sleep you would probably buy into the idea. When you are awake your dreams seem unreal to you (at least in memory), they seem like fantasy. The thought of utilizing a technique to alter your dreams seems plausible, because you do not associate dreaming as being real. This is where you are wrong. There is absolutely no difference between your waking reality and the reality of your dream world. Both realities are equally as tangible as the (real world) and equally as fluid as the (dream world).

The dream world seems unreal to us only when we awake and attempt to review our dreams with our conscious mind. Because we are not using our conscious mind when we dream, we do not have to process any of the information linearly. We also do not have doubt and rational thinking interfering. Our dreams can be wild and they can jump around from one universe to another far

Manifesting Techniques

off universe in a non-linear fashion and yet maintain the integrity of the reality within the dream. Upon wakening however, our conscious mind tries to make sense of the dream putting the pieces back together in continuity and suddenly we find the dream to be just unacceptable. Without our conscious mind interfering, we can manifest anything we want in our waking reality and the experience will remain completely real to us. It is our conscious mind that tries to regulate the rendering of the universes. It tells the subconscious mind that it "can't", and it tries to organize the events in a practical linear order. In reality, you can do anything you want if you can just quiet down the orders being given by your ego.

Because both realities are dream like, I have begun to wonder if our visualization technique should employ symbolism. Symbolism might be the preferred language to illustrate to our subconscious mind what we want in the same way that our dreams do when we are asleep. We often have bizarre dreams. Sometimes we might dream about snakes chasing us or dream that we're drowning or perhaps we're doing something completely out of context with our normal waking lives. Sometimes we try to make sense of the dreams because we think our dreams are trying to tell us something. For instance, Carl Jung suggested that being chased by snakes could symbolize a fear of death, drowning could symbolize getting in over your head or having too many problems. Whatever the symbolism is, I wonder if symbolism itself is the preferred language of the subconscious.

I read a story about a woman who utilized visualization techniques to beat cancer. The doctors told this woman she had no

Becoming God

chance of survival. Instead, they told her chemotherapy might give her an extra month or two at the most. She said that every time she sat in the chair to receive her treatment she would visualize her white blood cells moving throughout her body. Then she visualized the white blood cells as white bunny rabbits hopping around within her body and the rabbits are eating away at her cancer. The cancer, she imagined as an orange object and the white rabbits just couldn't get enough. The rabbits would eat the orange cancer (the carrots) and then multiply into more rabbits until there were more rabbits than there were carrots. Eventually, she imagined a bunny rabbit eating the last carrot. In her waking reality, the woman went into complete remission. Not a trace of cancer was to be found in her body.

She implemented symbolism in her visualization technique rather than trying to visualize an accurate picture of cancer cells and white blood cells. She chose white bunny rabbits to symbolize her white blood cells because rabbits multiply quickly and used carrots as a symbol for the cancer to create the perfect food for the rabbits to eat. Reading this got me thinking that this maybe a better way or if anything, another method of visualization. Sometimes we dream realities that are so incredibly real and yet other times we dream realities thick with symbolic references. I do not yet know which of the two methods would be most effective.

Most importantly, the use of meditation and visualization is not an activity it is a way of life. It is not something you try it is something you practice. You should make time for it everyday. Nothing you do in life can remotely have the same impact if you truly believe in the powers that lie dormant within you.

Visualization can be practiced in many ways. It can be something as simple as making a quick list of your goals and as you write them down you see them come to fruition in your minds eye. Find a quiet time for yourself each day to focus on your reality. Imagine what it looks like to travel within the vast Multi-verse and imagine that you are at the helm of the wheel. Find this time because nothing else is more important. Find this time because for you it is all that is real.

The Law of Attraction

I touched briefly on the Law of Attraction in Chapter 8 describing the effects of this principle when set to a default mode. By default we tend to react to our experience rather than take control of our experience. When things go wrong we tend to get sucked into our experience and dwell on the negative aspects of what we are experiencing. By default our subconscious interprets our focus as desire and takes us to different universes that full-fill our conscious requests. In other words we "attract" more of what we are focused on. The Law of Attraction simply suggests that any conscious being attracts their "external" experiences by thinking about them. To put it more simply you get out of life exactly what you expect to get. Expect greatness, luck, health, happiness, wealth and that is what your reality will be. Expect misery, failure, disappointment, betrayal, poverty and disease and this is what your world will become.

To understand how any of this could have any scientific

Becoming God

basis, we need to understand another aspect of quantum physics called "String Theory". String Theory is a complicated concept, which we could think about simply as a collection of vibrating strings representing un-rendered possible universes within the Multi-verse. At risk of sounding too meta-physical, we could think about these vibrating energy fields as strings vibrating either positively or negatively and, the law of attraction suggesting that positive vibrating strings are attracted to other positive vibrating strings "positive vibes" and negative vibrating strings are attracted to other negative vibrating strings "negative vibes". We often hear people talk about increasing "good or positive energy" in our lives and eliminating the people and experiences evoking "negative or bad energy". As hocus-pocus as this may sound, there is now some compelling science to suggest that there may be something to this. If we are to manifest experiences that evoke negative energy (negative feelings or "bad vibes") this is likely to attract other negative experiences. Consequently, if we consciously make determined choices to evoke, or manifest positive experiences we are more likely to attract other positive experiences.

Less scientifically, many believe (myself included) that these vibrations are representative of another sense that makes up the human experience and that sense is our emotions. Emotions are a factor that carry huge influence over the human experience however have little, if any scientific measurability. Nonetheless, their importance to our overall experience may be greater than the other senses combined and more than this, they just may be another key to self-awareness. Much of our conscious decisions are based on our feelings. We tend to go in the direction of things that make us feel good and steer clear of situations or experiences that make us feel bad. Remember, the mind does not distinct between "good" or "bad", there is no way for the mind to know that loosing your wallet is a bad thing, but it does know that it didn't make you feel good.

Applying this concept to positively manifesting your reality is quite simple. It starts with going towards the things that make you feel good and steering clear of things that make you feel bad despite the influences in your life directing you otherwise. This is sometimes easier said then done, but this is essential to manifesting the life that you desire. We may desire to have a happier life but if we are inundated with negative people, negative surroundings and experiences whether we want them or not we are going to attract more negative experiences. If, on the other hand, we want to attract more positive influences and experiences into our life we need to align ourselves with more positive situations which are likely to attract more positive experiences. By feeling good all the time and surrounding ourselves with people and experiences that inspire us and make us feel good we will attract more of the same. It is sometimes hard to eliminate people from our lives that we care about, but if they are riddled with drama and bad things are always happening to them, you need to find away to gracefully reduce your contact with them. The people around us can bring us up and elevate us to heights we never imagined or they can suck us down into the abyss of bad experiences. There is an old saying that says "misery loves company" now there is a concept that supports this.

On the contrary, it is not hard at all to feel good inside and to attract good and positive experiences. There are plenty of ways to find happiness without having material things. One simple way to feel good is through giving. When we give it makes us feel great. Giving doesn't have to cost you anything. Giving can be something as simple as a compliment. It is within this self-congratulatory happiness that you will attract more pleasurable experiences to your own life. Giving is receiving.

Dreams

Since the dawn of human reasoning, man has contemplated the meaning of his dreams. Nearly every culture throughout history has regarded their dreams as something sacred and of significant meaning. Though our dreams rarely make sense to us, we cannot deny their importance to our survival. Without them we would die.

When someone is deprived of R.E.M sleep, a condition of deep rest where the mind enters a dream state and the eyes begin a shimmering pattern called rapid eye movement (R.E.M.), we find that the physical and mental health of the person deteriorates at staggering levels. After just 96 hours of R.E.M. deprivation the person looses most, if not all of their mental faculties. They are unable to make cognitive responses; they experience frequent hallucinations, and loose nearly all of their coordination and motor skills. They also have a very bad time trying to distinguish reality from fantasy.

So what is happening to us when we dream? Dreams have been clinically studied for more than century now and still nobody knows for certain. What we do know is that it is only during our dreams, particularly the gamma wave state, that our brain is most active.

There are some who believe that when we dream we are either downloading or uploading daily information. Information either gathered by us for upload or information from somewhere else downloaded to us. This would make sense with the new understanding that the superconscious (our collective mind) processes and delegates information outside of the human body. There are others who believe that our dreams are moments when the observer pulls out of the body, the virtual interface, to either rest or refuel. This is consistent with the Aborigine Indians who believe that in our dreams we unite with God, that it is only within our waking reality that we have a separate ego and identity. Many believe there are messages in our dreams in the form of metaphors and symbols to instruct us to consciously re-direct our lives. Of course, there are others who believe that our dreams mean nothing at all. They believe dreams are nothing more than random thoughts firing off by neural connectors and it is our conscious mind that is trying to make sense of the chaos when we first awake.

Not to cop-out on this, but I think all of these ideas maybe true. I believe that there is both some purpose and meaning to our dreams but I also believe that our dreams are equally meaningless and random. I have no doubt that some of our dreams are trying to tell us something. But I also think that the messages come to us thick with symbolism and unless you are very good at playing charades it is difficult to recognize all of the metaphors.

Becoming God

  Carl Jung was the pioneer of recognizing metaphors within our dreams. He suggested that our dreams are filled with symbolic references and metaphors as both representations of desires or burdens in our waking life, as well as solutions and direction to our subconscious mind.   For example, a dream that you are being chased by snakes could be a metaphor for anxiety in your waking life. This dream represents our primordial fight or flight response. If you get away from the snakes in your dream, this might be a suggestion that you should avoid the current stress in your waking life. Turning back to fight the snake may be a metaphor for you to face your anxiety. The metaphor suggesting that your anxieties are nothing to fear and that you will overcome them by simply facing them head on. Some suggest that a dream of drowning represents unresolved personal issues such as a relationship ending badly or childhood fears left unresolved. Many psychologists believe that before you will be able to move on in your waking life, these issues need to be resolved. On a brighter note, many of us have had dreams of flying. It is suggested that this metaphor represents personal achievement, and control over your life. However, if you are having trouble staying aloft or if you run into trees or mountains or something of the sort, this could mean that someone or something is standing in the way of your aspirations.

  Whether or not these metaphors really have something to do with our waking reality I don't know. What is important here is to use your dreams as practice to recognizing metaphors in your waking life. There are no coincidences in your waking life because your are the master of your reality. If we regard our waking life as a dream, we could look for metaphors placed within our waking reality by our subconscious self for all of the guidance we could ever need. We should learn to trust our intuitions, ask for guidance out loud and act on metaphors when we uncover them in our waking life. Instead we have been incorrectly taught throughout our lives to regard any striking occurrence and merely coincidence. We are taught not to look too deeply into them. This advice could not be any worse. These incredible things happen because this is your minds way of telling you to pay attention. Looking for metaphors is the single best way to constantly remind yourself that you are dreaming in your waking life. Acting on them is the single greatest way to take control of your waking dream. Look for metaphors and you will find them everywhere. It is within the metaphors that you will find the guidance to anything you desire.

There is a practice of becoming aware that you are dreaming within the dreams of your sleep called lucid dreaming. Lucid dreaming is a technique where you become consciously aware that you are dreaming within your dream allowing you to take conscious control over your subconscious experience. It is said that you can then manipulate your dream by sheer will alone. Through lucid dreaming we can learn how to consciously become aware of our waking dream state and consciously take control of our lives to unlimited ability. Since I first learned about this practice a few years ago, I have only been able to do this once. I find this practice intriguing but very difficult to achieve. In my single lucid dream, I became aware that I was dreaming within my dream but I was still unable to manipulate it. The mere awareness to the fact that I was dreaming was enough interference to bring the dream to an end.

Becoming God

To practice lucid dreaming there are some clever techniques that you can employ to achieve a lucid dream state. Although, the practice of lucid dreaming is exactly that, practice. Lucid dreaming requires dedication, and patience but the result of this may very well have a profound impact on our waking reality. One suggestion to lucid dreaming is getting in the habit of reading text twice in your waking reality. It is said that any text within in a dream will never appear the same way twice and recognizing this may be enough to remind you that you are dreaming. Another suggestion is doing things in your dream that you would expect to give you feedback. For example, making an attempt to adjust the light while dreaming. You can do this by turning on a lamp or opening a curtain. In your dream, the light switch flicks or the curtains open but the surrounding light does not change, an indication that you are dreaming. Another practice is repeatedly looking at your hands in your waking reality. Make a habit out of looking at your palms and then the backside of your hands in your waking life and then attempt to do this while dreaming. Almost never can we see our hands when we are dreaming. It is suggested that often times the mind has difficulty producing our hands while we are dreaming which can be another indication that we are dreaming.

Upon awakening in your dream and achieving a lucid state of mind, it is suggested that you can direct the experiences of your dream and alter the reality within it. If you want to fly away, you simply think about it and do it. If you want to make flowers grow on the wall then simply make a wish and watch it happen. The power and ability you have during your lucid dream is nothing less or more than the powers you have in your waking life. You have the ability, just as in your lucid dream to alter the reality around you by sheer will alone. But, just as in the lucid dream, first you must become aware that you are dreaming and second, you have to believe that you can alter your dream. Think of your life as a dream, and when you sleep, think of your dreams becoming a dream within a bigger dream. If you can manipulate your dreams when you sleep, then you can manipulate your reality. Lucidly controlling the dreams of your sleep is in itself a metaphor, that we do have the ability to lucidly control the dream of our waking life.

Surrendering your ego

Giving up all that is you is probably impossible for anyone. However, with any luck, reading this book has opened your mind to the consideration of the true meaning of your life and to the possibility that your identity and your ego are merely illusions of grandeur. If you accept the main points of this book, then you are already on your way to reducing the significance of yourself as an individual and on to the realization that you are God; a God that is creating ego's to contemplate ideas. As humans, we create an alternate ego within our own minds every time we think about anything at all. We ask a question in our mind, and a voice (an alternate ego) answers the question. It is important to keep in mind that "you" are neither the voice asking the question in your mind nor are "you" the voice answering it. Instead, the part that is "you" is the one who is aware of the conversation.

Becoming God

We are all more than just connected; we are all a single conscious being creating multiple egos for both company and to express our thoughts and ideas through conversation. You are not just connected to other beings, you *are* the other beings and you are connected to reality itself because reality is something that you just made up. Think of your ego as a costume that our mind is putting on to experience something new and to learn something about itself. Think of reality as a world for the costume to "play" in to make the experience ever more real.

It is important to remember that everything you have ever experienced is a part of you. Every person you know, every starving child you saw on TV, as well as the TV itself and the couch you sat on while you watched it; they are all you. They are your thoughts and since thoughts are all that we are, you and the thoughts that created your reality are one and the same. Thoughts *are* things. Everything in the universe is nothing more than an idea, but just because ideas are not made of matter doesn't make them any less real.

"Row, row, row your boat
Gently down the stream.
Merrily, Merrily, Merrily, Merrily,
Life is but a dream."

~ Eliphalet Oram Lyte

Chapter 11:
Conclusion

Defining The Dream, Defining God

Seven years ago my skeptical Atheism would have balked at any of these ideas. In fact, it wasn't until very recently that I had this personal eureka and made the connection between meta-physics, positive suggestion, spirituality and the Multi-verse theory. It was this eureka that was the inspiration for this book. Once I had fully grasped the concept, I decided right then to change my life. I decided to pursue every inclination or urge that came to my mind regardless of the out come. If my mind was sending me a message I was going to embrace it and see it through.

I had an idea one night that I was supposed to write this book. I have never written anything other than a song in my life and I had no clue of how to begin. The old me, would have dismissed the idea of writing a book, especially a book about science and spirituality. Who the hell am I? I am not a scientist nor do I consider myself spiritual! But instead I embraced the idea. As irrational as it seemed at the time, my subconscious mind was telling me to write a book and so I did. I picked up my laptop and I have not stopped writing or researching this book since. I could have embraced the idea and said to myself, "Someday I will do it." But somehow I knew following these instructions *now* is what my subconscious mind was navigating me to do as the first step into achieving the other things I had hoped and dreamt for.

I began by visualizing myself researching data and staying up late at night typing into my laptop. I also visualized the finality of this project and my visualization included every detail. I visualized getting this book published, seeing it on bookstore

Conclusion

shelves and being bought and read by you. As ridiculous as it may sound, I visualized myself talking about this book on Oprah. In fact, it was a dream of discussing this book on Oprah that gave me the title. In my dream, I saw her holding the book up to the camera lens and saying the title, "Becoming God". It was the first time I had ever considered a title for the book (I had then hardly begun) and I did not give the title a second thought after that. That was what I envisioned the very first time and I never second-guessed it. I went with where my mind was taking me because I *knew* that whatever my mind could imagine would eventually manifest itself within my reality. By accepting the fact, that this glimpse was an actual reality for me to take, I chose to direct myself toward it making the reality ever more real. It would be nearly a year before my chosen title made any sense to me. Writing this book enabled me, in many ways, to grasp these concepts further than even I had ever grasped them before. It wasn't until well after writing this book that I realized the perfect way to describe the nature of reality is that we (or it) is in a constant state of "becoming". We are already "ONE", (a single consciousness) perpetually becoming new egos, new situations, new environments, new everything. It is in this constant state of becoming in which we learn something new about ourselves and further contemplate our own existence by comparing the various experiences that we become. I realize now that I couldn't have chosen a more perfect title.

This book is just the first step to forever changing my life. There is no doubt in my mind this book will be published and read by you. There is no doubt in my mind by writing this book I have changed the course of my reality. I have changed the direction of my dream and now I have opened the floodgate to a slew of new kinds of experiences. Galileo once said: *"You cannot teach a man anything; you can only help him find it within himself."* If I have succeeded in this then I have succeeded in my intention.

Since this is the conclusion of the book, I feel like I would be cheating you if I didn't offer some personal opinion about the theories presented in this book and their philosophical repercussions. As I mentioned before, it would infuriate me to no end when I would come to the end of some book about Quantum Mechanics and the author/scientist would not offer his or her philosophical intuition. I on the other hand, do have the advantage of freedom of expression without scrutiny from colleagues. After all, I am just a musician with a curiosity about the meaning of life. My career does not hang in the balance of anyone's thoughts of my opinions so long as it comes packaged in a catchy tune. With that being said, it is important to remember that my opinions are no more important or more correct than any opinions you may have about the subject. These are opinions about the unknowable, and there isn't anything that I can learn about in this world that could in anyway make me understand the meaning of life or what happens to us when the dream of waking life is over.

From everything I have read and everything I have considered on my own, I believe we are living within a dream. I believe that our waking reality is the expression of the possibilities of our imagination that exceed our comprehension. Life is a vacation from the mind, Gods' mind.

Conclusion

I believe that in both our waking reality and in the dreams of our sleep we are subject to an ego that is in place to convince us that we are somehow separate from everything else. I do not believe that we are. It is our ego that has us convinced that we are the subject of the experience rather than the creator of the experience. Our egos' skew our understanding not only in waking life, but in our dreams as well. In both realities we are convinced that we are somehow just a passenger with little ability to influence the events that are "happening" to us. However, with understanding and discipline we can awaken from our ego, find liberation from our fears and consciously take control of our experience in both the dreams of our sleep and the dream of our waking reality.

I believe in God. I believe that God is the dream of everything that is and ever will be. God is a thought, a supposition. God is what the universe is when it thinks. We are the thoughts of God. We are pure imagination being expressed and appreciated through the eyes of a conscious ego. When the thought is complete, the ego will cease to exist and our lives will seemingly be over. Egos are important. Egos help God consider a thought from a different perspective. What better way to learn the effects of something than to experience it first hand from multiple perspectives and points of view? I believe when we die, we slip back into a dreamless world absent of any meaning at all. I hope that when we die and shed the ego we have come to love, we will be granted comprehension of all thought. I know that in that moment all of the pain and loneliness experienced in this life would be worthwhile. In that moment we would awaken into a world where nothing matters at all, a world of all knowing bliss.

Becoming God

In that moment we would consciously become aware that we are God, and we would revel and laugh at the simplicity of it all, a simplicity so deep that in the absence of everything we would experience an apathetic euphoria incomprehensible to us now.

When I think about this simple place, I think about existence in its simplest form, a universe absent of any stress or worry and a universe absent of any goals or ambition. At the end of everything nothing matters at all, right or wrong we are merely a thought in an endless sea of thoughts. I started to think about this as an ideology and I wondered if a simple life might be the intended life for us in this waking reality. According to The Law of Attraction, If we just lived for now, this instant, and our only thought was for happiness then that thought or visualization would have to manifest itself in the next moment; a moment of subsequent happiness. No matter what, if we focused on happiness, the next moment would have to produce happiness regardless of what was seemingly happening around us. In order to manifest happiness, which is now the goal that our subconscious mind is visualizing and focusing on, everything would have to just "work itself out" to continue to produce happiness. Focusing on happiness and contentment are the ingredients to a euphoric, blissful experience. If happiness is what we are searching for, then all we have to do is ask for it. This practice of life seems to be not unlike the practices of the monks, who typically live in peaceful surroundings ever appreciative of the splendor of life. This is an admirable way to live, but in my opinion, to truly appreciate happiness we must sometime encounter struggle which is the very reason why we create a less than perfect life.

Conclusion

So far in this book we have addressed every question except for *why* which I would like to propose to you now:

We exist to raise the conscious level of God. Our lives are the mechanism for which God sorts out new understanding. Life is where God goes while his mind tries to comprehend his endless imagination. In other words, God is constantly blowing his own mind and life is where he/she/we/it go to ponder these notions through expression. Everything in life is a metaphor (a clue or a sign) to remind us not to get sucked into this false reality. *This is supposed to be fun!* As we begin to comprehend our new ideas we also begin to recognize the signs and metaphors we placed within the dream as a reminder to wake up, to become self-aware that we *are* God expressing and contemplating a new idea.

You might then ask; if we are dreaming what is our purpose in it all? I think our purpose is to act as the voice with which God reasons and contemplates anything and everything. As I said previously, when we think about anything in our own minds, at least three separate egos are involved; two to propose and answer the questions, and one to be aware of the conversation and ponder the ideas being discussed. I believe that "our" (individual egos) purpose now is to consummate three (3) goals so that we can recognize the final metaphors in our ascension to higher consciousness. It is not a coincidence that these are the three necessary qualities you must embrace within yourself before this book will make any sense to you, a book that I now believe is a metaphor in itself to help us wake up. These three goals are:

Becoming God

1. Open mindedness (one must acknowledge that their current train of thought is not the answer and one must be completely open to a new way of thinking)
2. Embrace benevolence through self-awareness (do good be good)
3. Liberation from all of our fears (have trust or faith)

Being open minded to new ideas, especially philosophies widely outside of your "box" of knowledge and previous experience, is absolutely necessary to raising your level of consciousness. More than this, you must be willing to accept that your current train of thought is not working. If it were, the world would be a perfect place and you would be experiencing everlasting happiness. This world is a wonderful place and I am very happy over all, but even I can admit there is still room for improvement.

Secondly, we must embrace benevolence. This simply means that we must always do the right thing towards ourselves and to others. With the understanding that we are one, we must treat others with the kindness, respect and compassion that we would expect for ourselves. Being kind to others makes us feel good about ourselves because they are us and we are them. Despite the distorted view your ego is giving you, it is important to always remember that we are a single conscious being trying to find our way in the barren of infinity. We must have tolerance towards "other egos" and be appreciative of our surroundings. Nobody is superior to anyone because we are one. Each of us is on our own predetermined journey; each with our own purpose and set of circumstance to serve our single source. Remember, everything you see around you is an extension of you.

Finally, facing what fears us most is how we begin the process of experiencing new ideas. Anything new is scary the first time; but if we recognize that fear is an illusion, then we can quickly find a way to grow from the experience. I can recall the first time I got behind the wheel of an automobile. It was a terrifying experience but it was also liberating at the same time. I understand now that facing my fears of driving a car required responsibility, but the reward from freedom of exploration was worth every bit of it. We should regard our lives exactly the same way. We will only become appreciative of our exploration if we remember what it took to overcome our fear of it in the beginning.

Until you recognize and embrace these three qualities or "Arthas" you will never be able to awaken from the dream. Reincarnation takes place when we have not obtained these three Arthas within the span of a single lifetime. This is my variation on the Hindu and Buddha religions. In fact, I believe that all of the religions have got a piece of the puzzle, and that we left metaphors within the scriptures of each one. Along with this, the Christians too are very close in saying that you must accept Jesus Christ as your savior before you will be allowed in the Kingdom of Heaven (a higher state of consciousness). Where the Christians have got it wrong is they misinterpreted this metaphor as believing that Christ (The Man) died for our sins. He did not, because there are no sins to forgive; there is only experience. Instead, we must believe in *The Way* that Jesus described to us in his teachings. Jesus was trying to teach us to become self-aware, but he was murdered before the lesson was completed. I understand this now because of the struggles I have encountered in writing this book. The only way to teach these concepts is in baby steps. In-small progressive increments are the only way to comprehend this new revelation, a revelation of Gods' mind. God is not awe, but Ah-ha!

I am now convinced that we left huge metaphors everywhere for ourselves to remind us of where we came from and how we should regard our lives. For example, if I were to describe the structure of God or come up with a symbol that best describes the nature of ultimate reality, the picture would look a lot like a tree. The tree is a metaphor, a constant reminder of who we really are. The trunk and root system of the tree would represent our source, our "oneness" from which we branch out into individual leaves (or lives) each of "us" encapsulated within our own reality to gain a different perspective. Each leaf is independent from the other leaves, but they are connected through our source. Together we feed and nurture our source by collecting water and energy from the sun. When our job is complete (The thought is over) the leaf dies and falls to the ground only to decompose so that it can once again be re-absorbed back into our source helping the tree to expand and grow.

We can communicate with our source whenever we choose. We can ask any question of our source, the answers to which will always be revealed to us through metaphor, recognizable only if we choose to believe in them. When I asked to understand the nature of ultimate reality, and what our role is in this mesmerizing dream I

Conclusion

found my answer oddly enough through the metaphors within <u>The Wizard of Oz</u>. After careful consideration, I began to write down my thoughts on what our purpose should be now to raise the conscious level of our source. As I began write down the words: *open mind, benevolence,* and *liberation from fear,* I was suddenly reminded of how these metaphors have been engrained in my psyche since childhood. In the movie, Dorthy is sucked into a tornado from her farmhouse in Kansas where she awakens in a ridiculous place called Munchkinland, a fantastical world of make believe. In this dream world, Dorthy desires to go home (to awaken from the dream). She learns that in order to get home she must go see the "Wizard" (the metaphor being God- her inner self) who will grant her any wish. Dorthy sets out on a yellow brick road (a metaphor for our metaphors) leading her to the Wizard who lives in a place called Oz. Along the way she encounters a living scarecrow who is in search of a brain (he has an open mind) who accompanies her to see the Wizard who may grant his wish. They next encounter a Tin Man who is in need of a heart (benevolence, compassion) who also accompanies them to see the Wizard. Next they encounter their third and last disciple, a Lion without any courage who yearns to face his fears.

Along the way, a Wicked Witch terrorizes them. Their fear of this Wicked Witch is almost enough to hinder them from completing their journey. Their struggle is a metaphor for life. If it were easy, they would not appreciate it. Finally, the four barely make it to their destination where they inevitably meet with the Wizard. Disappointingly, the Wizard tells them they must go back and get the broomstick of the Wicked Witch and bring it to him before he will grant their wishes. He tells them that they must face their fears. The four main characters oblige and face their most dreaded fear only to find that the Wicked Old Witch could be destroyed with a harmless glass of water (something that the human body is mostly made of; the metaphor being they had it within them all along). Amazed with their accomplishment and no longer afraid of anything, they have an effortless journey back to Oz and once again encounter the Wizard. It is during this encounter, and with their newfound courage, they realize that the Wizard is just a simple man hiding behind a curtain of almighty disguise (a metaphor for religion). When they ask the Wizard why he would do such a thing, the Wizard admits that he just wanted to see if they could do it (Experience). The Wizard tells the four they did not have to come all the way to Oz to have their wishes granted; but they had the ability to do it themselves all along. The scarecrow always had a brain; he just didn't believe that he was smart. So, the Wizard gives him a diploma, an accolade from the University of E Pluribus Unum (Latin for oneness), to remind him of his genius. The Wizard reminds the Tin Man that just by showing compassion for his friends and following his desires, he has a heart; and he gives the Tin Man a token to remind him. The Wizard then tells the Lion that he was always courageous; he just didn't know he had it in him to face his fears. And lastly, Dorthy discovers she could have gotten home any time she wanted. All she had to do was believe that she could. The reason she was told to set out on such a perilous journey was so she would discover newfound appreciation for her home. Dorthy clicks her heels *three* times to awaken from the dream safely back in her bed again in Kansas.

These are just a few of the dozens of metaphors I found in The Wizard of Oz, and this movie is just one of hundreds of metaphors (or "signs") that I have recognized within my life in the last several weeks. Now that I believe in their significance, I find them everywhere. These metaphors have filled my life with laughter and joy unlike anything I have ever experienced. The metaphors in my life are my yellow brick road. As long as I stay on it I will never be lost. Finding metaphors in your life is going to be a wonderful way for you to break down your barrier of doubt too. At first, you will dismiss the metaphors as coincidences, but somewhere in the back of your mind you will entertain the possibility. With increasing metaphors too fantastic to be coincidence you will begin to recognize that you are manifesting those metaphors into existence by thinking about them and looking for them. Within this realization you will discover that you *are* God and you will then know that you can do much more than merely manifest coincidences.

It is important for my readers to know that this book is not about quantum physics, nor is this book about religion. If this is what you have taken from this book, then you have missed the point. The preceding chapters are in fact metaphors to bring us to this final conclusion. This book is about becoming self-aware; aware that we are God, an idea that shatters everything we have come to understand about our lives and the world around us. Embracing this concept is not going to be easy for you. It wasn't

Becoming God

for me. I realize now that <u>The Search For Schrödinger's Cat</u> and further anomalies in quantum physics are just another metaphor; a sign or a clue that I left for myself, a symbol that did not set right with my psyche. This was one of the earliest metaphors that I recognized. Achieving my dreams was the first. The signs are so obvious now I can't escape them even when I try. There *is* something more to coincidence and there is nothing wrong with believing in this. Thus far we have ignored coincidences and look what it has brought us. What do you have to loose by changing your opinion now? What wonderful things do you have to gain by eliminating your doubt and having a little faith? God is beginning to comprehend his previous thought. I am (God is, you are) ready to wake up. Stop hitting the snooze button!

Take a deep breath and count to three… The concepts of this book are very difficult to accept. I highly recommend that you re-read this book several times over. A lot of the ideas I have presented here require multiple reviews before your conscious is going to allow it to penetrate your mind. Don't get discouraged if you are grasping only parts of this book. The entire picture will require effort, careful study and contemplation. Remember the clue you left for yourself; the Bible also infers: *It will be revealed to you in God's time.* Well, You are God! You will "get it" when you have comprehended it and not a second sooner. To fully comprehend anything you have to experience the lesson. For example, just as clichés and metaphors are used in everyday language, we really don't comprehend them until we experience them first hand. Then, at that moment, we say to ourselves, "Ah-ha! Now I get it."

Conclusion

Comprehension requires the elimination of doubt. Doubt will block these ideas at every level. To overcome this, I highly recommend doing your own research. Be a skeptic. Read other books, research this stuff on the Internet, look for your own metaphors, open a dialog with others and work your way through it; after all we are one. More important than anything however, is that you engage in conversation about these ideas. For it is within the conversation (saying it out loud and *teaching* it) that we begin to comprehend it. Until we say it out loud, for our own ears to hear, it's only an idea. As strange as this sounds, even I couldn't fully comprehend my book until I began to teach it. This book is simply divine. The metamorphosis that you received by reading this book is exactly the same one as I received while writing it. I began this book as an atheist and now I believe in God as I believe in my self. At the very least this book provokes the ultimate questions and makes us comfortable questioning paradigms.

Understanding this book will not be easy. This is okay; this is part of the comprehension process. I cannot tell you how many times I have tried explaining these concepts to people and in the middle of my description I got lost myself somewhere in the philosophy and had to go back and research it to firmly grasp the concepts again. These ideas and this philosophy are counter-intuitive and your brain is going to reject it at every level. Don't just read this book. *Think* about the concepts I have presented to you.

As unbelievable as these philosophies may be, they are all that we have and it is necessary that we contemplate them. They are the only philosophies that show *truth* with what I do know:

Becoming God

That we are dreaming; that unless we are observing it directly, reality has only the potential for existing and the dream is limited only by our imagination. Life is anything you want it to be and as detailed as you want to make it. The reality around us becomes real only when *we* choose to make it real. That is a powerful notion. You have the power to make anything of your life that you wish. What great thing would you do today if you knew you were going to die tomorrow? What greater things would you do if you knew there was no chance of failure? Regret at the end of your life means that you lost the game. Are you playing to win or are you playing to get all the way through it and loose? Are you playing to learn and experience all that is possible or are you playing a conservative game to come back and do this over and over until you have whole heartedly accepted this ideology and made the most of your experience? This is the discovery to end all discoveries. Discovering these concepts for yourself and embracing them makes this simply the most profound moment of your life.

What are you going to do with it?

"We are messengers sent from ourselves to ourselves to remind ourselves that we are worthy of asking the next question. It is within the answer of your next question that you will ascend to the next level of consciousness. There are no limits to the levels of ascension, for we will always have another question, the answer of which resides within our own imagination. For imagination evolves by supposition."

~ Lisa Ann Fordyce

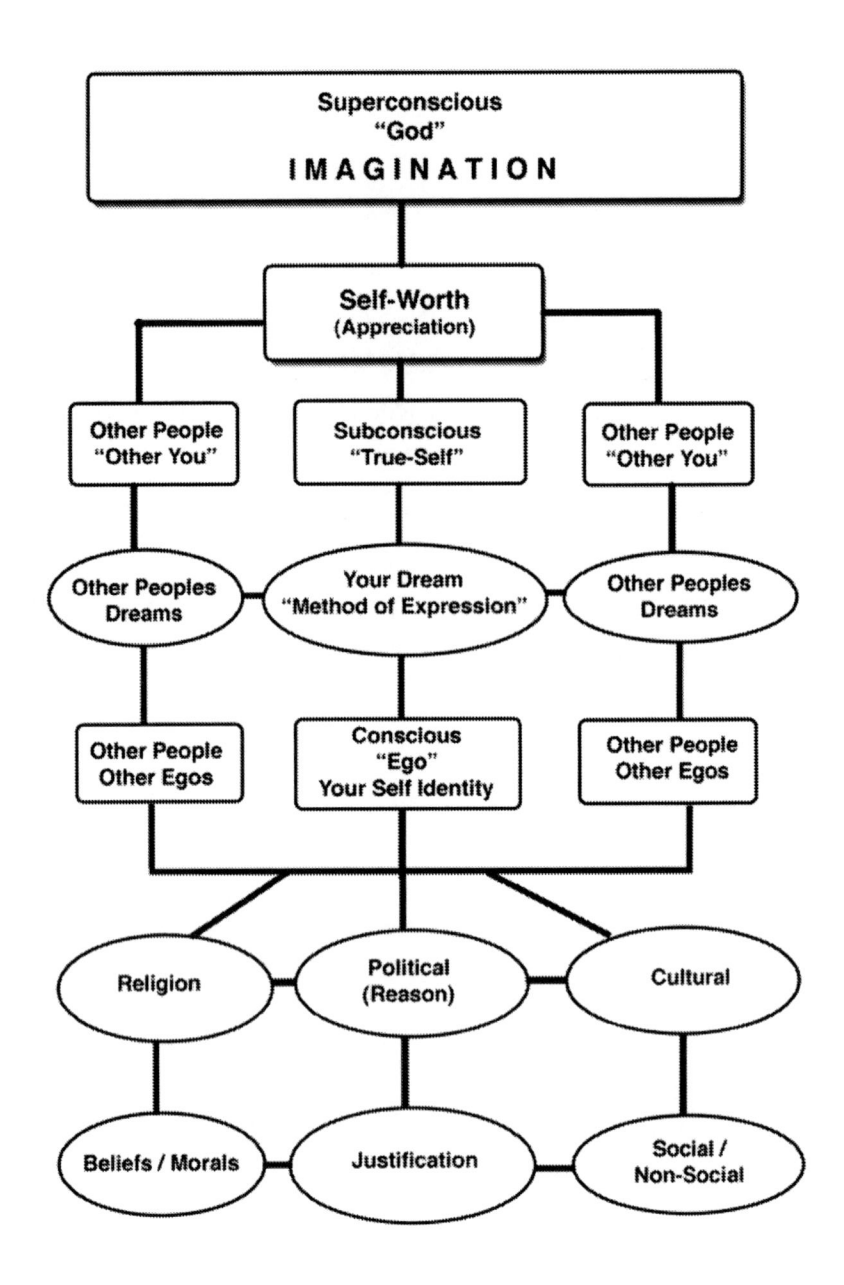

```
                    Superconscious
                         "God"
                     IMAGINATION
                           │
                    Self-Worth
                    (Appreciation)
          ┌────────────┼────────────┐
    Other People   Subconscious    Other People
    "Other You"    "True-Self"     "Other You"
         │              │               │
   Other Peoples    Your Dream     Other Peoples
      Dreams      "Method of         Dreams
                  Expression"
         │              │               │
   Other People    Conscious       Other People
   Other Egos        "Ego"         Other Egos
                 Your Self Identity
          └────────────┼────────────┘
       Religion      Political       Cultural
                     (Reason)
         │              │               │
   Beliefs / Morals  Justification   Social /
                                    Non-Social
```

© 2007 Drof Publishing

Time Chart

"PAST"	"PRESENT"	"FUTURE"
Experiences That We Have Already Comprehended	Events That We Are Experiencing Now	Experiences We Have Imagined But Have Yet To Comprehend
Thoughts Expressed	Current Expression	Changing Expression "Growth"

-------> Illusion of Time Flowing ------->

-------> Illusion of Time Flowing ------->

Resources

Books

In Search of Schrödingers Cat
John Gribbin
Bantam, 1984

The Fabric of Reality
Dr. David Deutsch
Penguin Books Ltd., 1998

Billions & Billions
Dr. Carl Sagan
Ballantine Books/ Random House, 1997

The Holy Bible
The New King James Version
Containing The Old and New Testaments

The Demon Haunted World
Dr. Carl Sagan
Ballantine Books/ Random House, 1996

The Power Of Your Subconscious Mind
By: Dr. Joseph Murphy, DRS, PHD, DD, LLD
Bantam revised, 2001

Hyperspace
Dr. Michio Kaku
Oxford University Press, 1994

The Mind of God
Dr. Paul Davies
Orion/Touch Stone, 1993

Psycho Cybernetics
Dr. Maxwell Maltz
Pocket Books, 1969

Mass Dreams of The Future
Dr. Chet B. Snow
McGraw Hill, 1989

The Dreaming Universe
Dr. Fred Alan Wolf
Simon & Schuster, 1994

The Search For Infinity
By Gordon Fraser, Egil Lillestol, Inge, Sellevag, Stephen Hawking
Facts On File Publishing, 1995

The World of Tibetan Buddhism
By: The Dalai Lama
Wisdom Publishing, 1995

Stephen Hawkings Universe
By David Filkin
Basic Books/ Perseus Books, 1997

Pale Blue Dot
By Dr. Carl Sagan
Ballantine Books, 1997

Cosmos
By Dr. Carl Sagan
Simon & Schuster, 1960

The God Particle
BY: Dr. Leon Lederman
Delta/ Dell Pub. Bantam Doubleday, 1993

Idiots Guide to Hypnosis
By: Dr. Roberta Temes
Alpha Books, 2000

1001 Smartest Things Ever Said
By Steven D Price
The Lyons Press, c. 2004

Short Story
"The Last Question"
Isaac Asimov
c.1956 from "The Best Of Isaac Asimov", 1973

Articles
'Multi-verse Theory' Holds That the Universe is a Virtual Reality Matrix
Sydney Morning Herald | July 22 2004

Scientific Papers
"Are You Living In A Computer Simulation?"
By Dr. Nick Bostrom
Philosophical Quarterly, 2003 Vol. 53, No. 211

"Many World's Quantum Theory"
By Michael Clive Price
c. 1995

"A Quantum Mechanical Model of The Human Brain"
By Dr. Granville Dharmawardena
Purify Mind

Online Courses
Kabbalah One
c 2004 Kabbalah Centre International